国际胜任力英语系列

国际胜任力
英语教程
——国际传播

总主编 王 昊

主 编 李玲玲

副主编 王浦程 高亚娟

清华大学出版社
北 京

内 容 简 介

《国际胜任力英语教程：国际传播》是一本以培养全球胜任力人才为核心目标的创新型英语教材。本书以全球治理议题为主线，通过案例分析、讨论等形式，帮助学生深入理解全球治理的复杂性和多样性。本书围绕全球治理环境议题展开，聚焦气候变化、生物多样性、水资源等八大领域，通过丰富的国内、国际真实案例并结合短视频制作等数字化项目实践，全面提升学生解决全球议题的综合素养、跨文化交际能力和国际传播实操能力。本书每个单元配套音频资源，读者可先扫描封底"文泉云盘防盗码"解锁资源后，再扫描书中对应处的二维码获取听力资源。

本书使用对象主要是高等院校的本科学生，也适合其他英语爱好者自学使用。

图书在版编目（CIP）数据

国际胜任力英语教程：国际传播 / 王昊总主编；李玲玲主编 . -- 北京：清华大学出版社，2025.2（2025.4 重印）.
（国际胜任力英语系列）. -- ISBN 978-7-302-68228-8

Ⅰ. H319.39

中国国家版本馆 CIP 数据核字第 2025LD1563 号

责任编辑：徐博文
封面设计：李伯骥
责任校对：王荣静
责任印制：沈　露

出版发行：清华大学出版社
　　　网　　　址：https://www.tup.com.cn, https://www.wqxuetang.com
　　　地　　　址：北京清华大学学研大厦 A 座　　　　　　邮　编：100084
　　　社 总 机：010-83470000　　　　　　　　　　　　邮　购：010-62786544
　　　投稿与读者服务：010-62776969, c-service@tup.tsinghua.edu.cn
　　　质量反馈：010-62772015, zhiliang@tup.tsinghua.edu.cn
印 装 者：三河市龙大印装有限公司
经　　销：全国新华书店
开　　本：185mm×260mm　　　　印　张：7.5　　　　字　数：175 千字
版　　次：2025 年 2 月第 1 版　　　　　　　　　　印　次：2025 年 4 月第 2 次印刷
定　　价：59.00 元

产品编号：103911-02

"国际胜任力英语系列"以《大学英语教学指南（2020版）》为指导，对接《中国英语能力等级量表》，落实立德树人根本任务，以中国特色的全球治理理念和实践为蓝本，探讨人类命运共同体等本土理念对全球性问题的贡献，旨在培养熟悉党和国家方针政策、了解我国国情、具有全球视野、熟练运用外语、通晓国际规则、精通国际谈判的国际化应用型人才。本系列教程通过讲好中国故事、融合学科交叉和探索实践新技术三方面，积极应对党和国家对新时代、新技术和新发展背景下的人才培养需求，即"为谁培养人""培养什么样的人"和"怎样培养人"的问题。本系列教程在内容上一方面体现全球治理的重要议题，帮助学生了解当今国际社会所面临的共同问题，拓宽学生的全球视野，培养跨文化交际能力；另一方面，结合学生实际需求，选择难度适中的语言材料和相关话题，各单元之间体现了递进性和连贯性，使学生能够循序渐进地掌握英语技能和知识。本系列教程以任务为导向设计真实情境下的交际任务，激发学生的学习兴趣。练习任务包括听力、口语对话、阅读理解、写作等，帮助学生将语言运用到实际情境中。

本系列教程积极回应新文科建设，以中国价值为核心，主动将中国智慧有机融入全球治理视角下的国际议题，通过学科交叉进行新知识生产体系的构建，在加深学生领悟本土价值的同时也提升了全球胜任力。本系列教程涵盖多个全球治理相关学科和领域的内容，使学生全面了解全球治理的多维度和复杂性，有效提升学生的跨学科知识素养。新文科建设回应科技文明的进步，将传统文科与技术的互动作为其核心之一。本系列教程在任务设计、素材选取、语言处理等多方面推进人文与技术的互动融通。具体而言，本系列教程以数字技术和人工智能为方法和手段，为学生构建大学英语教育新形态，将全球治理相关内容与英语语言知识和技能有机结合，在教授语言的同时还通过相关学科内容的介绍和讨论，拓展学生的学科知识面，形成一定的学科意识，提升学科语言能力。通过内容语言在顶层设计和教学实践中的创新性融合，本系列教程旨在培养学生的全球治理学科知识、语言能力。同时，从全人教育的视角，提升学生的世界观、人生观和价值观等个人素养。

教程特色

本系列教程引导学生拓展全球视野、理解多元文化交流场景中的语言使用习惯和跨文化交际技巧，通过引入大量的实践案例，如国际组织的运作机制和全球共性问题的应对措施等，一方面使学生了解不同国家和地区在全球治理中的角色和影响，另一方面帮助学生在国际交流中更加自信、更加有效地表达自己。本系列教程依托多媒体技术，采用以学为中心的设计思路，引入任务式、项目式和跨文化交际等多元学习形态，鼓励学生开展课内外、校内外和国内外的多维度合作学习，打造全方位、多元化的大学英语教育体验。

本系列教程共三册，分别为《国际胜任力英语教程：国际理解》《国际胜任力英语教程：国际传播》《国际胜任力英语教程：国际交流》。本系列教程的编排借鉴内容语言融合教育理念，主张语言知识技能和跨学科知识素养的综合培养。在主题设计方面，《国际胜任力英语教程：国际理解》涵盖八个主题：脱贫、教育、创新、和平、公正、道德、健康、全球公民；《国际胜任力英语教程：国际传播》涵盖八个主题：全球气候、资源可持续、水资源、物种多样性、森林砍伐、自然灾害、废物回收、绿色发展；《国际胜任力英语教程：国际交流》涵盖八个主题：政府间国际组织、非政府间国际组织、演讲技巧与礼仪、国际交流与合作、国际学术研讨、国际学术会议、国际学术合作、学术伦理与诚信。每个单元设定明确的教学目标，包括语言技能（听、说、读、写、译）、语言知识（词汇、语言功能）、交际能力（听力理解、口语表达、阅读理解、写作表达）、课程思政等。

编写团队

本系列教程由浙江外国语学院应用外语学院的核心教师团队组成编写组，学院教学副院长担任编写组组组长，院长助理和系主任担任主要编写人员，明确每一层级权责分工，定期举行主要编写成员间的编写交流会议。同时，编写组邀请校外长期从事大学英语教材编写的专家担任学术顾问。本系列教程从主题内容的初步构想、编写大纲的制定，再到书稿的细致审校，均得到了清华大学出版社领导及编辑团队的大力支持。在此，我们对他们表示衷心感谢。

鉴于编者能力所限，教程中可能仍存在疏漏与不足之处，我们诚挚地邀请广大师生不吝赐教，为本系列教程的完善提出宝贵意见和建议。

编写组

2024.3

CONTENTS 目录

Unit 3   Water Resources....................................29

Unit 4   Biodiversity 41

Unit 1

Climate Change

Quiz 1

Learning Objectives:

After studying this unit, you should be able to

- develop a comprehensive understanding of climate change on a global scale;
- recognize and respect cultural diversity in addressing global environmental issues;
- understand the themes, objectives, and guidelines of the course project.

PART **I** Listening and Speaking

Section 1 Pre-Listening Activity

Directions: *Discuss the following questions with your classmates. List the key information, and prepare to share your opinion with the class.*

(1) How would you describe the level of awareness about climate change in your community or country?

(2) In what ways do you believe climate change is affecting our daily lives?

(3) Why do you think international cooperation is crucial in addressing global climate issues?

(4) How can governments encourage the adoption of renewable energy in their respective countries?

(5) How effective do you think current government policies are in addressing climate change?

(6) In your opinion, how can education play a role in raising awareness of climate change?

Section 2 Listening Comprehension

Passage 1

1. Directions: *Listen to Passage 1 and choose the best answer to each question.*

(1) When was the Paris Agreement adopted, and how many parties adopted it?

    A. November 4, 2015, 196 Parties.

    B. December 12, 2016, 150 Parties.

C. December 12, 2015, 196 Parties.

D. November 4, 2016, 150 Parties.

(2) What is the overarching goal of the Paris Agreement regarding the global average temperature increase?

A. Well below 1.5°C.

B. Well below 2.5°C.

C. Well below 2°C.

D. Exactly 2°C.

(3) Why have world leaders stressed the need to limit global warming to 1.5°C in recent years?

A. It is the maximum limit allowed by the Paris Agreement.

B. The UN's Intergovernmental Panel on Climate Change recommends it to avoid severe impacts.

C. It aligns with the economic and social transformation goals.

D. It is the easiest target to achieve.

(4) What is the deadline for greenhouse gas emissions to peak according to the Paris Agreement?

A. 2020.   B. 2025.   C. 2030.   D. 2050.

(5) How does the Paris Agreement work to combat climate change?

A. It enforces immediate and drastic measures on all nations.

B. It establishes a yearly cycle of climate action based on decreasing ambition.

C. It works on an increasingly ambitious climate action by countries.

D. It relies on voluntary actions without any binding agreements.

Passage 2

1. Directions: Listen to Passage 2 and choose the best answer to each question.

(1) What is the primary purpose of the new regulations regarding straw burning in China?

A. To promote traditional farming methods.

B. To increase agricultural production.

C. To reduce air pollution and improve rural air quality.

D. To encourage open burning for easier disposal.

(2) When did China implement a strict ban on burning straw?

    A. 2020.   B. 2018.   C. 2015.   D. 2023.

(3) Why is the issue of burning straw more severe in China compared to Western countries?

    A. Western countries have larger populations.

    B. China has smaller agricultural production.

    C. China has large population and massive agricultural production.

    D. Western countries do not have strict regulations.

(4) What are the two environmentally friendly methods suggested for straw disposal?

    A. Open burning and landfilling.

    B. Recycling and incineration.

    C. Composting and returning straw to fields.

    D. Dumping in rivers and burying.

(5) How does composting contribute to improving soil quality?

    A. It adds more pollutants to the soil.

    B. It increases the emission of pollutants.

    C. It transforms straw into organic fertilizer over time.

    D. It has no impact on soil quality.

2. Directions: *Listen to Passage 2 again and decide whether the statements are true (T) or false (F).*

(6) _____ Western countries do not allow the burning of straw without proper controls.

(7) _____ China's ban on burning straw is primarily based on considerations of economic development.

(8) _____ Returning straw to the fields enhances soil structure and increases soil fertility.

(9) _____ The Chinese government implemented strict controls on burning straw due to a small agricultural production.

(10) _____ Both China and Western countries are actively exploring methods to reduce the environmental impact of burning straw.

PART **II** Reading and Speaking

Reading 1　What Has China Done to Address Global Climate Challenges?

More than 70,000 delegates from around the world were gathering in Dubai for the 28th meeting of the Conference of the Parties (COP28), the United Nations climate change conference scheduled from Novermber 30 to December 12, 2023. This meeting, convened under the United Nations Framework Convention on Climate Change, would be a milestone where the international community took stock of progress made on implementing the Paris Agreement.

China had halved carbon dioxide emission per unit of GDP, becoming a global leader in utilizing green and low-carbon energies, and actively promoting international cooperation on climate governance. Erik Solheim, former under-secretary-general of the UN and former executive director of the United Nations Environment Programme, told Xinhua Press that strong environment calls from the people, dedication from China's political leadership and innovations of Chinese businesses together made all these possible.

In 2022, China's carbon dioxide emissions per unit of GDP had dropped by more than 51% since 2005. The proportion of non-fossil energy consumption had reached 17.5%, and national forest coverage rate reached 24.02% in 2021. China has incorporated carbon emission reduction goals into overall economic and social development planning, pledging to peak carbon emissions by 2030 and achieve carbon neutrality by 2060. A national carbon market had been established, with cumulative transaction volume of carbon emission allowances reaching 238 million tons nationwide by the first half of 2023.

With total installed capacity of renewable energies reaching 1,213 gigawatts in 2022, China had become a global leader in utilizing green and low-carbon energy sources. The country had ranked first in the world for eight consecutive years in production and sales of new energy vehicles, with 16.2 million on the roads by June 2023. COP28 President-Designate Sultan Ahmed Al Jaber noted that China is the key in the decarbonization of today's energy, as a powerhouse producing the majority of the world's solar panels, wind turbines and lithium-ion batteries.

China is active in promoting international cooperation on addressing climate challenges and has been deeply engaged in South-South cooperation in this regard. By June 2023, China had signed 46 climate change memorandums of understanding with 39 developing countries, launched over 70 mitigation and adaptation projects, and helped train more than 2,300 officials and technicians from over 120 developing countries.

China jointly established a **ministerial** conference mechanism for climate action with the EU and Canada in 2017. In August 2023, China and the United States released The Sunnylands Statement reaffirming their commitment to work together and with other countries to address the climate crisis.

China has been promoting climate change cooperation under the Belt and Road Initiative (BRI) **framework**, providing support for other developing countries. In the first half of 2023, 56% of China's overseas energy investment in BRI countries went into renewable energy projects.

 New Words

delegate	/ˈdelɪgət/	n.	代表；会议代表
milestone	/ˈmaɪlstəʊn/	n.	里程碑；重要事件
innovation	/ˌɪnəˈveɪʃən/	n.	创新；革新
proportion	/prəˈpɔːʃən/	n.	比例；部分
non-fossil	/nɒnˈfɒsɪl/	adj.	非化石的
pledge	/pledʒ/	v.	保证；誓言
neutrality	/njuːˈtrælɪti/	n.	中立；中立状态
cumulative	/ˈkjuːmjʊlətɪv/	adj.	累积的；渐增的
allowance	/əˈlaʊəns/	n.	配额；津贴
renewable	/rɪˈnjuːəbl/	adj.	可再生的；可更新的
consecutive	/kənˈsekjʊtɪv/	adj.	连续的；连贯的
mitigation	/ˌmɪtɪˈgeɪʃən/	n.	缓解；减轻
adaptation	/ˌædəpˈteɪʃən/	n.	适应；改编
ministerial	/ˌmɪnɪˈstɪərɪəl/	adj.	部长的；内阁的
framework	/ˈfreɪmˌwɜːk/	n.	框架；结构

 Phrases and Expressions

carbon dioxide	二氧化碳
installed capacity	装机容量
Conference of the Parties (COP)	缔约方会议

the Paris Agreement	《巴黎协定》
green and low-carbon energy	绿色低碳能源
solar panel	太阳能电池板
wind turbine	风力涡轮机
carbon emission reduction goal	减排目标
national forest coverage rate	国家森林覆盖率
South-South cooperation	南南合作
memorandums of understanding	谅解备忘录
renewable energy project	可再生能源项目

Reading 2　EU Climate Cooperation with the Americas

The American continent accounts for one fifth of global greenhouse gas emissions, with two thirds originating from North America alone. Many countries in the region have yet to define their **decarbonisation** path. Emissions sources also differ, with North American emissions mostly from energy and transport, while in Latin America and the Caribbean (LAC), emissions mainly originate from land use and agriculture. The Americas are also home to countries that are very **vulnerable** to the climate change impacts. For these reasons, **engagement** and cooperation with the Americas is crucial to reach the Paris Agreement objectives.

In North America, cooperation with the US and Canada focuses on coordinating approaches to key global trade, climate and technology issues (via the EU-US Trade and Technology Council) and cooperation in the areas of climate, environment, clean energy **transition** and green industrial transformation (via the EU-Canada Green Alliance). The EU, US and Canada work closely to reduce greenhouse gas emissions, implement global **initiatives** (e.g. Global Methane Pledge), and advance research and innovation.

The EU's climate **diplomacy** engagement in Latin America and the Caribbean aims to promote the energy transition away from coal and other **fossil fuels**, enhance the use of renewables and **energy efficiency**, foster carbon markets, strengthen **resilience** to climate impacts and support nature-based solutions. Another key priority is preserving relevant **ecosystems** that constitute important **carbon sinks** in LAC countries, such as the Amazon rainforest, as well accessing the **critical raw materials** necessary for the green transition.

Climate cooperation initiatives with partner countries in the Americas include: the EU-Canada Green Alliance, Just Energy Transition Partnerships (JETPs) with the US and Canada through the G7, the EU-US Trade and Technology Council discussing climate, clean technologies, and green trade; the EU-US High-Level Climate Action Group (HLCAG) providing a platform for exchanges and outreach; and High Level Dialogues (HLD) on climate with Colombia, Mexico, Chile and Argentina in Latin America.

The EU and Argentina have increased cooperation on clean energy transition, energy security and raw materials. With Brazil, a High Level Dialogue on climate and environment has been launched, and the EIB has provided €300 million to Banco Santander Brasil for small-scale solar energy investments.

Recent engagements include: a speech by President von der Leyen at a high-level event on carbon pricing organized by Canada; the establishment of an EU-Canada Green Alliance; the first EU-Chile High Level Dialogue on Climate and Environment; a High Level Dialogue between Mexico and the EU on environment and climate policies; and joint press releases on the EU-US Trade and Technology Council and the Global Methane Pledge Energy Pathway.

 ## New Words

decarbonisation	/diːˌkaːbənaɪˈzeɪʃən/	n.	脱碳；减少碳排放
vulnerable	/ˈvʌlnərəbl/	adj.	易受伤害的；脆弱的
engagement	/ɪnˈgeɪdʒmənt/	n.	参与；合作
transition	/trænˈzɪʃən/	n.	转型；过渡
initiative	/ɪˈnɪʃɪətɪv/	n.	倡议；行动
diplomacy	/dɪˈplɒməsi/	n.	外交
resilience	/rɪˈzɪliəns/	n.	韧性；恢复力
ecosystem	/ˈiːkəʊˌsɪstəm/	n.	生态系统
outreach	/ˈaʊtˌriːtʃ/	n.	外展；推广

 ## Phrases and Expressions

solar energy	太阳能
greenhouse gas emission	温室气体排放
energy efficiency	能源效率
carbon sink	碳汇
raw material	原材料
clean energy transition	清洁能源转型

fossil fuel	化石燃料
renewable energy	可再生能源
carbon pricing	碳定价
critical raw material	关键原材料
EU-Canada Green Alliance	欧盟—加拿大绿色联盟
Global Methane Pledge	全球甲烷承诺
Just Energy Transition Partnership (JETP)	公正能源转型伙伴关系

Speaking Activity: Exploring Climate Change Initiatives in Intercultural Contexts

Step 1: Country Assignment and Preliminary Research

(1) Group A: Research China's climate change initiatives and cultural influences, such as the concept of "ecological civilization" and public support for environmental protection.

(2) Group B: Research the EU's climate change initiatives in the Americas, considering cultural influences in North America, Latin America, and the Caribbean.

Step 2: Multimedia-Rich Presentations and Interactive Q&A

(1) Group A: Present how Chinese cultural influences have shaped China's climate change initiatives, such as the pledge to peak carbon emissions by 2030 and achieve carbon neutrality by 2060.

(2) Group B: Present how cultural influences in the Americas have impacted the EU's climate cooperation efforts in the region, such as the environmental movement in North America and the importance of preserving the Amazon rainforest.

(3) Conduct a class presentation session with interactive Q&A, discussing how culture affects the implementation of climate policies and engagement strategies.

Step 3: Role-Playing Simulation

Organize a role-playing activity where Group A represents China and Group B represents the EU, negotiating potential collaborations and shared initiatives while considering cultural differences and similarities.

Step 4: Guest Speaker Interview

Invite a student acting as a guest speaker, such as a researcher who has studied the cultural dimensions of China's ecological civilization approach or an EU diplomat involved in climate cooperation with Latin American countries, to discuss how cultural factors shape the design, implementation, and effectiveness of climate change initiatives in different contexts.

Step 5: Present Findings and Engage in Class Discussion

(1) Write a reflective essay or journal entry on how cultural influences in China and the Americas shape the way people perceive and understand climate change initiatives. Think about how learning from different cultures can help the world work together more effectively on climate action.

(2) Reflect on how learning about China's holistic view of the relationship between humans and nature, or the EU's approach to engaging with different cultures, has expanded your understanding of how culture and climate change are interconnected. How has this knowledge broadened your perspective?

PART **III** Understanding Global Issues

Directions: *Discuss the following questions with your group members. Note down the key information and share your insights with the class.*

(1) What role have human activities played in recent climate change?

(2) How is climate change affecting different regions of the world?

(3) How might climate change impact global economies?

(4) How might technological innovations contribute to addressing climate change?

PART **IV** Developing Intercultural Communication Competence

Activity 1　Two Truths and One Lie

Directions: *Work in groups of four. Each group member should share three aspects of a culture—two truths and one lie—focusing on traditions, customs, food, language, or social norms. After each member shares, the group will discuss and try to identify the lie. Finally, the speaker will reveal the lie and provide explanations for the truths.*

For example:

- Truth: Hangzhou is home to the Grand Canal, the longest canal or artificial river in the world, and a significant historical landmark.

- Truth: Hangzhou is known for its traditional dish, Dongpo Pork, a slow-cooked braised pork belly named after the poet Su Dongpo.

- Lie: The Leifeng Pagoda in Hangzhou was originally built by the order of Emperor Kangxi during the Qing Dynasty to commemorate his visit to the city.

Activity 2   Metaphor Task

Directions: *A metaphor is a figure of speech that applies a word or phrase to an object or action in a non-literal way. First, read the text provided below and identify the metaphors used throughout. Then, explain what each metaphor represents and discuss the importance of respecting diverse cultures in understanding global environmental issues.*

Imagine our world as a big garden, where every country is a different plant. Some are big trees, some are small flowers, and some are bushes or grass. Just like a garden, our world faces challenges like changes in weather and running out of water. In some places, there are too many plants (or people) and not enough water. In other places, important plants (or animals) are disappearing. All the plants in our garden need to live together, but sometimes they compete for sunlight and water, like countries fighting for oil or land.

In the future, our garden will need more water (energy resources like oil and gas). Countries will have to talk and make deals about sharing these resources, especially in areas where it's not clear who owns the water or sunlight. It's like neighbors deciding how to share garden tools or water for their plants. Sometimes, they might need a garden committee (like the World Trade Organization) to help them agree. These talks are important because they help all parts of the garden grow well without fighting.

Our garden's weather is changing too. Some areas are getting too much rain, causing floods, while others are too dry, leading to wildfires. These changes can make it hard for plants to grow and animals to find food. For example, some parts of our garden, like coastal areas or small islands, might get flooded, and the plants (people) living there might have to move. The changing weather also brings new bugs and diseases, which can harm the plants. To protect our garden, all the gardeners (countries) need to work together, share their best gardening tips, and help each other.

To make our global garden thrive, gardeners from different parts of the garden (people from different cultures) need to talk and share their knowledge. Some might know how to save water, while others know how to protect plants from diseases. This is where talking to each other, understanding different ways of gardening (intercultural communication), becomes very important. By learning from each other, gardeners can find new ways to take care of their plants and keep the garden beautiful for everyone.

PART V Introduction to the Course Project

Project Description

As an essential component, you will be tasked with a project centered on making a short video. This project, scheduled for submission at the conclusion of the semester, provides you with a chance to present the distinctive viewpoints and attitudes of the contemporary youth in China. The short video should carefully delve into subjects associated with the earth, environment, humanity, and nature. As you get ready to participate in the forthcoming short video series, it is vital to concentrate on three essential elements: short video themes, objectives, and guidelines.

Themes: Be aware of the central themes the short video presents and you are encouraged to select and cover at least one of the following Unit Themes in our textbook in the short video. These themes are carefully chosen to enrich your understanding of the subject matter. Reflect on how these themes relate to the broader topic and your own experiences.

- Global Climate Change

- Resource Sustainability

- Water Scarcity

- Species Diversity

- Deforestation

- Natural Disasters

Objectives: As you make the short video, constantly refer back to the following objectives. They should guide the content, style, and approach, ensuring that the short video is not just a project, but a meaningful contribution to the understanding and action on environmental issues.

- To create opportunities for Chinese college students to express their understanding of environmental issues.

- To encourage the development of creative storytelling skills in an informative and engaging manner.

- To raise awareness and inspire action on crucial environmental challenges.

Guidelines: In order to ensure the quality of the short video, it is essential that you carefully produce the short video in accordance with the following requirements.

- **Length:** The short video should be 3–5 minutes in length.

- **Language:** English should be the working language in the short video. The voiceover work should be done by the students themselves. Also, the video should have subtitles in both English and Chinese.

- **Content:** The content of the short video must be focused and well-researched, presenting a clear and cohesive narrative on the chosen topic. Its content should revolve around a distinct theme, conveying positive, healthy, and uplifting messages.

- **Multi-media Use:** Incorporating relevant multimedia elements is highly recommended to enhance your presentation. These can include short video clips, micro-animations, concise educational videos, brief documentaries, micro-movies, music videos, and situational short films.

- **Originality:** Creativity and originality in the presentation will be a significant aspect of the evaluation.

- **Accuracy:** All information presented must be factually accurate and properly cited.

Unit 2

Sustainability

Quiz 2

Learning Objectives:

After studying this unit, you should be able to

● develop a comprehensive understanding of sustainability from a global perspective;

● recognize the importance of linguistic sensitivity for effective intercultural communication;

● identify and analyze the types and functions of digital genres in short videos.

PART I Listening and Speaking

Section 1 Pre-Listening Activity

Directions: Discuss the following questions with your classmates. List the key information and prepare to share your opinion with the class.

(1) How would you explain sustainable development to someone who is unfamiliar with the concept?

(2) Can you think of examples where sustainable development practices have been successful on a global scale?

(3) How can universities and educational institutions promote awareness and action towards sustainable development?

(4) How do you envision the future if sustainable development practices are not widely adopted?

(5) How can awareness and behavioral change be fostered among the general population?

(6) Can you think of any countries with effective policies promoting sustainability?

Section 2 Listening Comprehension

Passage 1

Directions: Listen to Passage 1 and choose the best answer to each question.

(1) What is the main focus of the Paris Agreement and the Sustainable Development Goals?

A. Economic growth.

B. Climate action and sustainable development.

C. Global political stability.

D. Technological innovation.

(2) According to the speaker, what is the key target of the Paris Agreement to limit global heating?

A. 2.5°C.   B. 1.0°C.   C. 1.5°C.   D. 3.0°C.

(3) What is the significance of the G20 in the context of greenhouse gas pollution?

A. It represents 20 countries aiming for sustainable development.

B. It is responsible for implementing the Paris Agreement.

C. It produces 80% of all greenhouse gas pollution.

D. It leads global efforts in renewable energy.

(4) The speaker mentions the "Great Green Wall" as an example. What is the main purpose of this initiative?

A. To create a physical barrier against climate change.

B. To promote tourism in Africa.

C. To restore degraded lands and combat desertification.

D. To build a wall of trees to stop wildfires.

(5) According to the speaker, what are the essential ingredients needed to fulfill the Paris Agreement?

A. Solidarity and technological innovation.

B. Money and green economic corridors.

C. Money and solidarity.

D. Global political stability and economic opportunity.

Passage 2

1. Directions: Listen to Passage 2 and choose the best answer to each question.

(1) Who is urging joint efforts on sustainability at Davos according to the news?

A. Du Jiangfeng.

B. A representative from the World Economic Forum.

C. Zhejiang University faculty.

D. The president of Harvard University.

(2) What role does Du Jiangfeng attribute to higher education institutions in tackling climate change challenges?

A. Financial support.

B. Conducting rigorous and actionable research.

C. Advocating for policy changes.

D. Hosting global forums.

(3) Which of the following universities is NOT mentioned as part of the Global University Leaders Forum (GULF)?

A. Tsinghua University.   B. Oxford University.

C. Peking University.   D. Stanford University.

(4) What is one of the key themes for this year's GULF, as mentioned in the news?

A. Advancing technology in education.

B. Exploring sustainable development.

C. Enhancing campus operations.

D. Promoting international collaboration.

(5) What did Zhejiang University release earlier this week according to the news?

A. A progress report on climate change.

B. Its first-ever Sustainable Development Goals report.

C. An annual financial statement.

D. A report on scientific research achievements.

2. Directions: *Listen to Passage 2 again and decide whether the statements are true (T) or false (F).*

(6) _____ Zhejiang University is the only Chinese university mentioned as part of GULF.

(7) _____ According to a UN progress report, all the Sustainable Development Goals are on track with their intended trajectories.

(8) _____ Zhejiang University faculty published research papers covering all 17 Sustainable Development Goals project areas in the past five years.

(9) _____ Du Jiangfeng suggests that universities should focus solely on conducting research to address the gaps in progress toward the Sustainable Development Goals.

(10) _____ The news mentions that the World Economic Forum's 54th annual gathering in Davos brought together over 2,800 participants.

PART Ⅱ Reading and Speaking

Reading 1　Beijing 2022—Innovative Solutions for a Carbon-Neutral Olympics

In line with the International Olympic Committee's requirements, Beijing 2022 implemented a range of measures to avoid and reduce carbon emissions. These efforts included minimizing construction by reusing five of the Beijing 2008 venues, powering all Games venues with renewable energy sources such as solar and wind, introducing low-carbon technologies, employing low-carbon transport, and creating forestry-based carbon sequestration projects.

The Zhangbei flexible direct current grid project, accelerated by the Games, used wind and solar energy to transfer electricity from Zhangjiakou to Beijing, supplying about 10% of Beijing's electricity consumption and boosting the city's use of clean energy. Additionally, natural CO_2 refrigeration systems, a low climate impact technology, were used at four Beijing 2022 ice venues, reducing carbon emissions from the cooling process to nearly zero while cutting heat waste and energy consumption.

The Games also served as a catalyst for regenerating city areas and accelerating regional development in the three competition zones: Beijing, Yanqing District, and Zhangjiakou. In Beijing, the Shougang Park, a former industrial area, was renovated and revitalized, transforming into a vibrant community where people live, work, and play. Yanqing saw a 35.2% growth in disposable income per capita between 2015 and 2019, leveraging its proximity to the Great Wall of China and the Beijing 2022 venues to become an all-year tourist destination. Zhangjiakou grasped the opportunity of the Olympic Games to promote ice and snow tourism and related industries, becoming China's largest ski resort and lifting all 12 poverty-stricken counties and districts out of poverty, benefiting 939,000 people in 1,970 villages.

Beijing 2022 was also the most gender-balanced Olympic Winter Games to date, with women accounting for 45% of the athletes. Gender balance was reached in several sports, and the Games featured the highest number of women's events ever, with the addition of women's **monobob**, women's big air skiing, and four mixed-team events, increasing the percentage of women's events in the Olympic programme to 47%.

The Games also ushered in a new era of transportation, with the Beijing-Zhangjiakou high-speed railway and the Beijing-Chongli highway reducing travel time between Beijing and Zhangjiakou from three hours to just 47 minutes. **Fuel-efficient** vehicles accounted for 100% of all passenger cars and 85% of all vehicles, with the Beijing Zone using mainly electric and natural-gas-powered vehicles, while the Yanqing and Zhangjiakou Zones deployed **hydrogen-fuelled** vehicles. Beijing's public transport also used intelligent bus dispatching systems, increased transfer parking lots, bus connections, and bicycle routes to improve transport efficiency and reduce carbon emissions.

 ## New Words

carbon-neutral	/ˈkɑːbən ˈnjuːtrəl/	adj.	碳中和的
construction	/kənˈstrʌkʃən/	n.	建设；建筑
forestry	/ˈfɒrɪstri/	n.	林业；森林管理
sequestration	/ˌsiːkweˈstreɪʃən/	n.	隔离；封存
refrigeration	/rɪˌfrɪdʒəˈreɪʃən/	n.	制冷
catalyst	/ˈkætəlɪst/	n.	催化剂；促使变化的因素
renovate	/ˈrenəveɪt/	v.	翻新；修复
revitalize	/ˌriːˈvaɪtəlaɪz/	v.	使复兴；使恢复生气
disposable	/dɪˈspəʊzəbl/	adj.	一次性的，可支配的
proximity	/prɒkˈsɪmɪti/	n.	接近；邻近
poverty-stricken	/ˈpɒvəti ˈstrɪkən/	adj.	贫困的；贫穷的
monobob	/ˈmɒnəʊbɒb/	n.	单人雪橇
fuel-efficient	/ˈfjuːəl ɪˈfɪʃənt/	adj.	燃料高效的
hydrogen-fuelled	/ˈhaɪdrədʒən fjʊəld/	adj.	氢燃料的

 ## Phrases and Expressions

carbon sequestration project	碳封存项目
ice and snow tourism	冰雪旅游

high-speed railway	高速铁路
electric and natural-gas-powered vehicle	电力和天然气驱动的车辆
intelligent bus dispatching system	智能公交调度系统
vibrant community	充满活力的社区

Reading 2　Paris 2024—Pioneering Sustainability at the Olympic Games

The 2024 Paris Olympic and Paralympic Games are set to make history as the most sustainable Olympics ever. The organizers have pledged to halve the event's carbon footprint compared to the average of previous Summer Games, despite the massive scale of the event, which will feature 800 Olympic sporting events, 15,000 athletes, 45,000 volunteers, and 13 million meals. To achieve this ambitious goal, Paris 2024 has developed a comprehensive sustainability strategy that incorporates a range of innovative measures.

One of the key ways Paris 2024 will reduce its environmental impact is by prioritizing the use of existing or temporary infrastructure. An impressive 95% of the events will be hosted in existing buildings or temporary venues, with only one new competition venue being built specifically for the Games: the solar-powered Aquatics Centre in Saint-Denis. The Athletes' Village will also be a model of sustainability, generating energy from geothermal and solar power, using mattresses made from recycled fishing nets, and incorporating biodiversity features such as rooftop enclosures for insects and birds.

The organizers are also taking steps to encourage sustainable travel and food choices during the Games. Paris 2024 has pledged to double the amount of plant-based food served and halve the amount of single-use plastic used, while also providing 1,000km of cycle lanes and making 3,000 more pay-as-you-go bikes available. Most Olympic venues will be accessible by public transport, making it easier for the 15 million visitors expected to attend the Games to make environmentally friendly travel choices.

To further reduce its impact, Paris 2024 is applying the "ARO" approach—avoid, reduce, then offset—along with two additional stages: anticipating emissions and mobilizing action. By accurately identifying the sources of emissions and proposing solutions for every activity, such as low-carbon structures, renewable energy, and sustainable catering, Paris 2024 aims to halve the carbon footprint of the Games compared to the average of previous Summer Games. Any emissions that cannot be avoided will be offset by projects designed to bring both environmental and social benefits on all five continents.

The **legacy** of the Paris 2024 Olympic Games is set to extend far beyond the event itself. The Athletes' Village will be transformed into a neighbourhood incorporating the best environmental standards, providing homes and workplaces for more than 12,000 people. The Games will also serve as a testing ground for more responsible solutions, inspiring progress in the world of sport and events well beyond 2024. Paris 2024, in collaboration with the French Ministry of Sport and the Olympic and Paralympic Games, the National Olympic and Sports Committee, and the French Agency for Ecological Transition (ADEME), has developed the "Events Climate Coach", a free online tool to help sports events in France reduce their carbon footprint, ensuring that the sustainability lessons learned from the Games can be shared and applied widely.

 ## New Words

comprehensive	/ˌkɒmprɪˈhensɪv/	*adj.*	全面的；综合的
sustainability	/səˌsteɪnəˈbɪlɪti/	*n.*	可持续性；持续性
infrastructure	/ˈɪnfrəˌstrʌktʃə/	*n.*	基础设施
temporary	/ˈtempərəri/	*adj.*	临时的；暂时的
geothermal	/ˌdʒiːəʊˈθɜːməl/	*adj.*	地热的
biodiversity	/ˌbaɪəʊdaɪˈvɜːsɪti/	*n.*	生物多样性
enclosure	/ɪnˈkləʊʒə/	*n.*	围场；封闭
plant-based	/plænt-beɪst/	*adj.*	植物性的；以植物为基础的
accessible	/əkˈsesɪbl/	*adj.*	可到达的；易接近的
offset	/ˈɒfset/	*v.*	抵消；补偿
anticipate	/ænˈtɪsɪpeɪt/	*v.*	预见；预计
mobilize	/ˈməʊbɪlaɪz/	*v.*	动员；组织
legacy	/ˈlegəsi/	*n.*	遗产；遗留问题

 ## Phrases and Expressions

sustainable Olympic	可持续奥运会
carbon footprint	碳足迹
geothermal and solar power	地热和太阳能
low-carbon structure	低碳结构
sustainable catering	可持续餐饮
Events Climate Coach	赛事气候指导

Speaking Activity: Sustainable Olympics and Linguistic Sensitivity

Step 1: Form Groups and Assign Roles

(1) Form groups of 4–5 students.

(2) Assign the following roles within each group: facilitator, note-taker, timekeeper, and presenter(s).

(3) The facilitator ensures everyone participates, the note-taker documents key points, the timekeeper keeps the group on track, and the presenter(s) share the group's findings with the class.

Step 2: Analyze and Compare Sustainability Measures

(1) Read Text A and Text B individually, focusing on the sustainability measures implemented in the Beijing 2022 and Paris 2024 Olympics.

(2) As a group, discuss and compare the sustainability initiatives in both Olympics. Consider the following questions:

● What are the main sustainability goals of each Olympics?

● How do they plan to reduce their carbon footprint?

● What innovative solutions or technologies are used?

(3) The note-taker should document the key points of the discussion.

Step 3: Explore Linguistic Sensitivity and Intercultural Communication

(1) Discuss how the texts present sustainability initiatives from different cultural perspectives.

(2) Consider how the language used in the texts might be perceived by people from different cultural backgrounds. Are there any terms or phrases that could be misinterpreted or offensive?

(3) Brainstorm ways to communicate sustainability initiatives effectively while being sensitive to different cultural perspectives. Consider the following:

● Using clear, concise language

● Avoiding jargon or culturally-specific references

● Providing context and explanations for culturally-specific concepts

(4) The note-taker should document the main points of the discussion.

Step 4: Prepare a Presentation

(1) Prepare a 5-minute group presentation on your findings from the previous steps.

(2) The presentation should include:

- A comparison of the sustainability initiatives in the Beijing 2022 and Paris 2024 Olympics

- Examples of how linguistic sensitivity and intercultural communication can be applied when discussing sustainability

- Suggestions for effective communication strategies when discussing sustainability with people from different cultural backgrounds

(3) The presenter(s) should deliver the presentation, with other group members contributing as needed.

Step 5: Class Discussion and Reflection

(1) After all the groups have presented, engage in a class discussion on the key takeaways from the activity.

(2) Reflect on how understanding linguistic sensitivity and intercultural communication can help promote sustainability initiatives globally.

(3) Consider how you can apply these lessons in your own life when communicating about sustainability with people from different cultural backgrounds.

PART Ⅲ Understanding Global Issues

Directions: Discuss the following questions with your group members. Note down the key information and share your insights with the class.

(1) What are the key challenges and opportunities in implementing sustainable development practices in both developed and developing countries?

(2) How can individuals contribute to sustainable development in their daily lives, and what lifestyle changes might be necessary to promote sustainability?

(3) What role do cultural and social values play in shaping attitudes and behaviors towards sustainability?

(4) In your opinion, what are the key challenges hindering global progress towards sustainable development, and what solutions or approaches would you propose to address them?

PART Ⅳ Developing Intercultural Communication Competence

Activity 1   Lost in Translation?

Directions: *Direct translation of words or phrases from one language to another can sometimes lead to misunderstandings due to differences in linguistic structures and cultural connotations (e.g., 四喜丸子、君子、江湖、韬光养晦). In your group, each member should share three phrases or sentences which they believe could be ambiguous or easily misunderstood when translated between Chinese and English. Discuss why these translations might be challenging and explore the cultural connotations behind them.*

For example:

- Every day at the café, she is in blue, sitting quietly in the corner with a distant look in her eyes.

- 留得青山在，不怕没柴烧。

Activity 2   Bridging Worlds Through Words

Directions: *Read the text below and engage in a discussion about the importance of linguistic sensitivity in cross-cultural communications.*

The digital age has brought a surge in cross-cultural interactions. From social media to global teams, our words now reach further and faster than ever before. In this digital age, the impact of our words is greatly magnified. A poorly chosen phrase in a social media post can quickly upset a large audience, making linguistic sensitivity not just a social nicety, but a necessity.

If we're not thoughtful with our words, small mistakes can turn into big problems. For example, in America, people might say "break a leg" to wish someone good luck. But, if a company uses this phrase in an international advertisement in a different country, people who are unfamiliar with the idiom might get confused. They might take it literally and think the company is actually wishing for someone to get hurt, which is not good!

This misunderstanding illustrates a broader issue: the way we talk can sometimes offend people from different cultures. In some countries, being direct and to the point is common and appreciated. However, in other cultures, such directness might be perceived as rudeness. This disparity highlights that effective intercultural communication involves more than just linguistic skill; it requires an understanding of cultural differences.

So, remember this: words are not merely words; they are potent tools that can bridge cultures. We must be culturally sensitive and mindful of how our words are interpreted by a global audience.

PART Ⅴ Introduction to the Course Project

Digital Genre

Digital genre refers to the strategic use of digital tools such as computers, smart phones, and other devices in recurrent, goal-directed, and communicative events, along with the assemblage of activities that surround these events. Thus, digital genres are inherently multi-modal and hybrid, including elements from various genres.

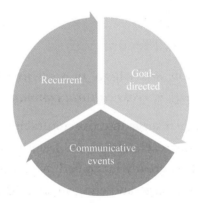

Short video is a popular form of digital genre that uses various digital tools to quickly engage and inform viewers on different platforms, showcasing a wide range of topics and styles. Here is a list of common genres in short videos:

(1) **Educationals/Instructionals**: Videos focusing on teaching or explaining concepts in various fields such as science, history, language learning, DIY projects, and cooking recipes. They are designed to be informative and concise.

(2) **Vlogs (Video Blogs)**: Personal vlog content where creators share aspects of their daily lives, travels, experiences, thoughts, and feelings. It is similar to a diary in video format. For example, videos showcase travel experiences, adventures, destination guides, and cultural insights from around the world.

(3) **Product Reviews and Unboxings**: Videos showcase the unboxing of products and providing reviews. They are commonly used in technology, beauty, and lifestyle sectors.

(4) **Documentaries/Informatives**: Short documentaries or informative clips that provide insights into real-life issues, events, or profiles of interesting people and places.

(5) **News and Current Affairs**: Short videos that provide updates on current events, news stories, and analyses of recent happenings.

(6) **How-To and Tutorials**: These videos focus on "how-to" instructions for various tasks, ranging from makeup tutorials to home repairs, crafts, and technology uses.

(7) **Public Service Advertisements:** These are public interest messages traditionally broadcasted by the media for free, aiming to increase awareness and influence public attitudes and behaviors regarding social issues.

Each genre serves a different audience interest and can be tailored for various platforms based on the content style and length preferences of the audience.

Unit 3

Water Resources

Quiz 3

Learning Objectives:

After studying this unit, you should be able to

- develop a comprehensive understanding of global water resources;
- develop the awareness of nonverbal communication for successful intercultural communication;
- identify and apply key video script elements for effective message delivery.

PART I Listening and Speaking

Section 1 Pre-Listening Activity

Directions: *Discuss the following questions with your classmates. List the key information and prepare to share your opinion with the class.*

(1) What are the main sources of water resources in the world, and how are they distributed geographically?

(2) How does having enough or not enough water affect your everyday life? Have you ever had a time when you were aware of needing to save water?

(3) How do human activities affect water resources? Discuss with examples such as agriculture, industry, and urban development.

(4) What role do governments and international organizations play in managing and protecting water resources? Discuss any successful policies or programs you are aware of.

(5) How is the climate change affecting water resources globally? Discuss the relationship between climate patterns and changes in water availability.

(6) Looking ahead, what are the biggest challenges and opportunities in ensuring sustainable water resources for all? How can everyone help solve water shortages?

Section 2　Listening Comprehension

Passage 1

1. Directions: Listen to Passage 1 and choose the best answer to each question.

(1) What was the primary cause of the floods in Pakistan, India, and Bangladesh in 2022?

    A. Melting glaciers.

    B. Monsoon season with higher-than-normal precipitation.

    C. Man-made dam failures.

    D. Sea-level rising.

(2) How much of Pakistan's total area was inundated due to the floods?

    A. About 5%.

    B. Roughly 9%.

    C. Approximately 18%.

    D. Over 20%.

(3) What was the economic loss due to flooding in Niger?

    A. USD 2 billion.

    B. USD 2.4 billion.

    C. USD 4.2 billion.

    D. USD 6 billion.

(4) Which region(s) faced a drought for the third consecutive year in 2022?

    A. The Sahel Region.

    B. Horn of Africa and Central Africa.

    C. La Plata Basin.

    D. Southern Asia.

(5) What was a significant impact of the drought in the La Plata Basin?

    A. Increase in river flows.

    B. Reduction in hydropower production.

    C. Improved crop production.

    D. Rise in groundwater levels.

Passage 2

1. Directions: *Listen to Passage 2 and choose the best answer to each question.*

(1) What is the primary significance of protecting water resources?

    A. To ensure water is available only for industrial processes.

    B. To sustain life, preserve ecosystems, and support economic growth.

    C. To increase the profitability of water-intensive industries.

    D. To limit water access to urban areas only.

(2) Why is the traditional approach to dealing with water issues considered impractical?

    A. Because it doesn't consider climate change.

    B. Because it focuses too much on economic growth.

    C. Because it separates water management from other natural elements.

    D. Because it doesn't involve community participation.

(3) What is the purpose of Integrated Water Resources Management (IWRM)?

    A. To restrict water usage by agricultural sectors.

    B. To balance economic, social, and environmental needs in water management.

    C. To prioritize industrial water use over ecological needs.

    D. To eliminate public participation in water management decisions.

(4) According to the Global Water Partnership, what does IWRM promote?

    A. Coordinated development and management of water only.

    B. Coordinated development and management of water, land, and related resources.

    C. Strict regulations on water usage.

    D. Economic growth at the expense of water resources.

(5) What is essential for achieving effective water protection?

    A. Technology.

    B. Regulations.

    C. A comprehensive strategy involving regulations, technology, and community participation.

    D. Solely community participation.

2. Directions: *Listen to Passage 2 again and decide whether the statements are true (T) or false (F).*

(6) _____ Water plays a minor role in the economic growth of societies.

(7) _____ IWRM is a concept that was developed solely based on theoretical studies.

(8) _____ The World Summit on Sustainable Development took place before Agenda 21.

(9) _____ The issue of water reservation gets complicated and crucial globally as population diminishes.

(10) _____ A comprehensive strategy for effective water protection involves regulations, technology, and community participation.

PART II Reading and Speaking

Reading 1   Water Resource Conservation Practices in China

China, as one of the world's most populous countries, faces significant challenges in water resource management due to its vast population, rapid industrialization, and environmental pollution. Recognizing the critical importance of water conservation, China has implemented a series of innovative and comprehensive strategies to protect its water resources.

One of the cornerstones of China's water conservation efforts is the "Three Red Lines" policy, which was introduced in 2011. This policy sets strict limits on water consumption, efficiency, and pollution levels. The first "red line" caps the maximum volume of water usage to ensure sustainable water supply, the second promotes the efficient use of water resources across all sectors, and the third mandates stringent controls on water pollution to protect water quality.

China has also invested heavily in water-saving technologies, particularly in agriculture, which accounts for a significant portion of the country's water use. Techniques such as drip irrigation, sprinkler systems, and the use of drought-resistant crops are being promoted to enhance water efficiency. In urban areas, rainwater harvesting systems and gray water recycling are increasingly being adopted to reduce freshwater demand.

The South-North Water Transfer Project is another ambitious initiative undertaken by China to address water scarcity. This megaengineering project aims to divert water from the water-rich south of the country to the arid north, including Beijing and Tianjin, to **alleviate** water stress in these regions.

Furthermore, China has made significant strides in enhancing its wastewater treatment infrastructure. The country is working to increase the capacity and efficiency of wastewater treatment plants to ensure that a larger proportion of industrial and residential wastewater is treated before being discharged into water bodies.

Public education and awareness campaigns are also a crucial part of China's water conservation strategy. The government and various NGOs are actively involved in educating the public about the importance of water conservation and encouraging sustainable water use practices.

 New Words

significant	/sɪgˈnɪfɪkənt/	adj.	重要的；显著的
conservation	/ˌkɒnsəˈveɪʃən/	n.	保护；保存
industrialization	/ɪnˌdʌstriəlaɪˈzeɪʃən/	n.	工业化
cornerstone	/ˈkɔːnəˌstəʊn/	n.	基石；基础
mandate	/ˈmændeɪt/	v.	强制执行；授权
stringent	/ˈstrɪndʒənt/	adj.	严格的；严厉的
drought-resistant	/draʊt rɪˈzɪstənt/	adj.	抗旱的
scarcity	/ˈskeəsɪti/	n.	稀缺；缺乏
arid	/ˈærɪd/	adj.	干旱的；贫瘠的
alleviate	/əˈliːvɪeɪt/	v.	缓解；减轻

 Phrases and Expressions

drip irrigation	滴灌
"Three Red Lines" policy	"三条红线"政策
drought-resistant crops	抗旱作物
rainwater harvesting system	雨水收集系统
gray water recycling	灰水/生活废水回收利用
South-North Water Transfer Project	南水北调工程
water scarcity	水资源稀缺
wastewater treatment	污水处理
public education and awareness	公共教育与意识

Reading 2   How Australia Is Securing Its Water Future

The **Millennium** Drought from 1996 to 2010 brought long-term water restrictions to Australia's highly populated southeast and southwest, acting as a catalyst for change. With the population in the cities predicted to grow by an additional 20 million people in the next 30 years, and water consumption expected to rise by 73% to more than 2,650 gigalitres, Australia is looking beyond its traditional rain-fed dams and reservoirs to secure its water future.

To meet the growing demand, Australia is turning to technology, with all mainland states investing in large **desalination** plants, each producing up to 674 gigalitres of additional freshwater. However, desalination is costly and controversial, consuming so much energy that its water is nicknamed "bottled electricity". In Western Australia, dwindling rains have decreased runoff into Perth's **reservoirs** by 91% since the 1970s, forcing an increased reliance on **groundwater**. To address this, Perth is actively replenishing its **aquifers** by pumping 10% of its treated wastewater into shallow aquifers that naturally filter and store the water until it is needed again, a process called Indirect Potable Reuse.

In addition to increasing water availability, Australia is also focusing on conservation. Many products are rated and labelled for water efficiency, and homes are increasingly adopting water-saving features. More than a quarter of Australian homes collect and store rainwater for domestic use, contributing around 177 billion liters to residential water supplies. Together with domestic wastewater systems that treat and reuse greywater, these integrated water management systems take pressure off **municipal** supplies for non-**potable** functions. Most cities restrict garden hosepipes and irrigation systems through voluntary Water Wise Measures, with Melbourne putting permanent rules in place that have almost reduced daily water consumption to a target of 155 liters per person.

In rural areas, where homes and communities often rely entirely on declining rains and diminishing groundwater, securing water can be expensive and complicated. Technological innovations, such as **hydro panels** that extract moisture from the air, may offer solutions for isolated locations. Agriculture, which consumes around 70% of Australia's water footprint, has also been the focus of more efficient and sustainable water management. The 2004 National Water Initiative committed state governments to reversing widespread overuse by agriculture, with the Murray-Darling Basin Plan covering the region responsible for most of Australia's food production. Water entitlements were bought from landholders to keep around 60% of the basin's water for the benefit of the environment and the long-term sustainability of supply, while billions of federal dollars have supported farm improvements to reduce water use.

The widespread acceptance that environmental sustainability is a crucial goal of water management is arguably Australia's most important change in water policy. Despite the progress made, many areas in Australia are still suffering from low rainfall and high temperatures, with major cities facing water restrictions and relying on desalination plants. This could be a major test of the plans, projects, and technologies put in place to **mitigate** the effects of drought, leaving everyone wondering if Australia has done enough to secure its water future.

 New Words

millennium	/mɪˈlenɪəm/	*n.*	千年
desalination	/diːˌsælɪˈneɪʃən/	*n.*	海水淡化
reservoir	/ˈrezəvwɑː/	*n.*	水库；蓄水池
groundwater	/ˈɡraʊndwɔːtə/	*n.*	地下水
aquifer	/ˈækwɪfə/	*n.*	含水层
municipal	/mjuːˈnɪsɪpl/	*adj.*	市政的；地方政府的
potable	/ˈpəʊtəbl/	*adj.*	可饮用的
entitlement	/ɪnˈtaɪtlmənt/	*n.*	权利；资格
mitigate	/ˈmɪtɪɡeɪt/	*v.*	缓解；减轻

 Phrases and Expressions

hydro panel	水面板；水力面板
millennium drought	千年干旱
water restrictions	限水措施
rain-fed dams	雨水供给的水坝
bottled electricity	瓶装电力
Indirect Potable Reuse	间接饮用水再利用
water wise measures	智慧用水措施
national water initiative	国家水资源倡议
water footprint	水足迹
Murray-Darling Basin Plan	墨累—达令盆地计划
environmental sustainability	环境可持续性

Speaking Activity: Promoting Water Conservation Public Awareness Campaign in Intercultural Contexts

Step 1: Form Groups and Assign Target Audiences

(1) Form into a group of 4–5 students.

(2) Each group will be assigned a target audience for a water conservation public awareness campaign (e.g., urban residents, rural farmers, industrial managers, etc.).

Step 2: Research and Brainstorm

(1) Groups research the water conservation strategies and challenges specific to their target audience, drawing from the texts about Australia and China.

(2) Brainstorm ideas for an effective public awareness campaign, considering the audience's cultural background and communication preferences.

Step 3: Develop Campaign Materials

(1) Each group develops a set of campaign materials tailored to their target audience, such as posters, brochures, social media posts, or short video scripts.

(2) Materials should incorporate culturally appropriate messaging, visuals, and nonverbal communication cues.

Step 4: Presentation and Feedback

(1) Each group presents their campaign materials to the class, explaining their rationale and how they addressed cultural considerations.

(2) The class provides feedback on the effectiveness of the campaign and offers suggestions for improvement.

Step 5: Reflect and Discuss

(1) As a class, discuss the importance of tailoring water conservation messages to different audiences and cultures.

(2) Reflect on how public awareness campaigns can be more effective when they consider the target audience's cultural background and communication styles.

PART **III** Understanding Global Issues

Directions: *Discuss the following questions with your group members. Note down the key information and share your insights with the class.*

(1) How can communities and individuals contribute to conserving water resources in their daily lives?

(2) What are the major challenges to water resources in your local area?

(3) What could be the main causes of water scarcity globally in the near future?

(4) How can we use technology to improve water conservation and efficiency?

PART **IV** Developing Intercultural Communication Competence

Activity 1   One Gesture, Dual Meanings

Directions: *Read the following passage and discuss its key points and themes. Could you provide more examples beyond those already listed?*

    Arab men often greet by kissing on both cheeks. In Japan, men and women greet by exchanging bows. Remember that the interviewer greets you with a simple handshake. In Thailand, to signal another person to come near, one wags one's fingers back and forth with the palm down. You will recall that the interviewer send you a beckoning message with her palm facing up. In Vietnam, that same motion is reserved for someone attempting to summon a dog. In Italy and various Arab countries, it is not uncommon for people to be thirty minutes tardy for an appointment. And there you were, making sure you were on time for your interview! Tongans sit down in the presence of superiors; in the West, you stand up, as you did with the interviewer. Crossing one's legs in the United States is often a sign of being relaxed; in Korea, it is a social taboo. In Japan, gifts are usually exchanged with both hands. Muslims consider the left hand unclean and do not eat or pass objects with it. The simple thumbsup used in the United States to say "okay" is an offensive gesture in Nigeria. The Buddha maintained that great insights arrived during moments of silence. In the United States, people talk to arrive at the truth.

Activity 2   Whispers Without Words

Directions: *Read the text below and engage in a discussion about the importance of nonverbal communication in cross-cultural communications.*

Nonverbal communication is a vital element in scriptwriting for digital media because it significantly influences the storytelling process and how the audience interprets the narrative. This form of communication encompasses a range of expressions beyond words, such as facial expressions, gestures, and body language. These nonverbal cues are essential for conveying emotions, intentions, and relationships quickly and effectively to a diverse audience. While some are universal, many are culturally specific. For instance, gestures that are considered polite or positive in one culture might be offensive in another. Scriptwriters must be aware of these differences to avoid miscommunication or cultural insensitivity. This awareness is crucial in intercultural communication within short videos, as the content may be consumed by a global audience. Scriptwriters need to either use universally understood nonverbal cues or carefully select culturally specific gestures that are explained or contextualized within the narrative.

Incorporating accurate and respectful representations of nonverbal communication from various cultures can enhance the relatability of short videos. Through subtle gestures, meaningful looks, or strategic uses of space and proximity, scriptwriters can add depth to their characters and complexity to their narratives, often without a single word being spoken. When viewers see their own cultural nuances reflected on screen, it can create a stronger emotional connection to the content. This inclusivity not only broadens the appeal of the video but also fosters a sense of understanding and empathy among viewers from different cultural backgrounds.

PART V Introduction to the Course Project

What Is a Video Script?

A video script is a written document that serves as a blueprint for the production process, guiding directors, actors, camera operators, and editors through the creation of the video. It ensures that all members of the production team are aligned with the video's objectives, storyline, and visual style.

In short videos, scriptwriting focuses on several key elements to effectively convey the message or story within a limited timeframe. These elements include:

- **Focus:** The core idea or message. What is the video about? What do you want the audience to take away from it?

- **Audience:** Consider who the video is for and what will engage them, paying attention to the nuances of intercultural communication across different cultures.

- **Clarity and Conciseness:** Every word and scene must serve a purpose. The script should get to the point quickly, avoiding unnecessary details or digressions.

- **Strong Opening:** The first few seconds are crucial to capture the audience's attention. A compelling opening is essential, whether it is an intriguing question, a surprising fact, or an emotional appeal.

- **Core Message:** The central idea or message should be clear and focused. In short videos, there is limited time to explore complex themes, so the script must communicate the core message efficiently.

- **Creativity:** Use creative techniques to stand out. Since short videos rely heavily on visual elements to engage viewers, the script should include detailed visual descriptions that complement the narrative and enhance the message.

- **Pacing:** The rhythm of the video needs to be carefully managed. The script should balance the delivery of information, ensuring that it is neither too rushed, which might overwhelm viewers, nor too slow, which could lose their interest.

- **Emotional Engagement:** Even in a brief format, connecting with the audience emotionally can make the message more memorable. The script should aim to evoke emotions through relatable situations, characters, or narratives.

Remember to share your script with your peers for feedback and be open to revisions. You may need to write multiple drafts and learn from each version.

Unit 4

Biodiversity

Quiz 4

Learning Objectives:

After studying this unit, you should be able to

- develop a comprehensive understanding of biodiversity on a global scale;

- recognize and analyze the vital role of context in intercultural communication;

- develop an on-site shooting plan tailored to your specific needs.

PART Ⅰ Listening and Speaking

Section 1 Pre-Listening Activity

Directions: *Discuss the following questions with your classmates. List the key information, and prepare to share your opinion with the class.*

(1) In your local area, what threats to biodiversity have you observed? How do you think these threats impact local ecosystems and communities?

(2) Using a real-life example, illustrate the importance of biodiversity for ecosystem stability and resilience. How does this example demonstrate the value of biodiversity?

(3) Can you share an example of a biological invasion and discuss the impact of the invasive species on local biodiversity and ecosystem function?

(4) What measures do you think can be taken to mitigate or prevent the damage to biodiversity caused by human activities? Provide some specific suggestions or solutions.

(5) Using a real-life example, discuss how climate change is altering biodiversity and ecosystem interactions, impacting species diversity.

(6) Besides the above questions, what other issues on biodiversity are you interested in, and why?

Section 2 Listening Comprehension

Passage 1

1. Directions: *Listen to Passage 1 and choose the best answer to each question.*

(1) What does the Kunming-Montreal Global Biodiversity Framework mainly aim to?

A. Increase industrial production.

B. Halt and reverse biodiversity loss.

C. Promote global trade.

D. Support space exploration.

(2) According to the passage, what percentage of species in studied animal and plant groups are at risk?

A. 10%.   B. 15%.   C. 25%.   D. 50%.

(3) What is the primary consequence if no action is taken to reduce the causes of biodiversity loss?

A. Biodiversity will remain stable.

B. The rate of species extinction will accelerate.

C. The rate of species extinction will slow down.

D. All species will adapt and survive.

(4) Which of the following is NOT mentioned as a main cause of change in nature?

A. Climate change.

B. Introduction of alien species.

C. Direct exploitation of organisms.

D. Global trade policies.

(5) At what rate does the report mention that biodiversity is declining?

A. Comparable to the past 10 million years.

B. Faster than at any time in human history.

C. Slower than expected.

D. Stable and unchanged.

2. Directions: *Listen to the passage again and decide whether the statements are true (T) or false (F).*

(6) _____ The Kunming-Montreal Global Biodiversity Framework involves only governments in its efforts.

(7) _____ The Global Biodiversity Outlook provides strong evidence that biodiversity is improving globally.

(8) _____ The biosphere is being altered across all areas on an unmatched level.

(9) _____ About 50% of species in studied groups are at risk of extinction.

(10) _____ The main causes of biodiversity loss are social values and behaviors.

Passage 2

Directions: *Listen to Passage 2 and fill in the missing words and sentences.*

The economic importance of biodiversity is vast, covering both obvious and hidden benefits that ecosystems provide to human societies and economies. Biodiversity supports essential ecosystem services crucial for human well-being and economic development. These services include pollination, soil (1) _____ maintenance, water purification, and climate (2) _____, which are fundamental for industries like farming, forestry, fishing, and (3) _____. They play a vital role in global economies.

Biodiversity is also a valuable source of (4) _____ resources, with many plants, animals, and microorganisms offering compounds used in medicine. These discoveries fuel innovation and growth in the pharmaceutical industry. (5) _____ diversity within biodiversity is essential for breeding programs aimed at improving agricultural productivity, resilience, and food (6) _____. Genetic resources from biodiversity significantly contribute to agricultural economies globally. Furthermore, biodiversity inspires innovation in biotechnology, leading to advancements in medicine, materials, and renewable energy. (7) _____ designs have practical applications in various industries. Tourism benefits from biodiversity-rich areas, drawing millions of visitors each year. National parks, wildlife (8) _____, and natural landscapes generate income through tourism activities, support local economies and creating jobs. Biodiversity also has cultural and (9) _____ value, shaping the identity and traditions of indigenous communities worldwide. These connections enrich tourism experiences and help preserve cultural (10) _____.

Moreover, biodiversity provides resilience against environmental disasters and climate change. (11) _____

_____. In conclusion, recognizing the economic value of biodiversity emphasizes the need to conserve and manage it sustainably. (12) _____.

PART **Ⅱ** Reading and Speaking

Reading 1　Biodiversity Conservation Practices in China

Biodiversity refers to the variety of living species (plants, animals and microorganisms) in their natural environments and the aggregate of the related ecological processes. It is measured on three levels: genes, species and ecosystems. Biodiversity is the basis for human survival and development and has a direct bearing on our wellbeing. Humans must respect nature and follow its ways. We must conserve biodiversity to protect nature and live in harmony with it.

In 1972, at the United Nations Conference on the Human Environment, the attending nations signed the *Declaration of the United Nations Conference on the Human Environment*, which included the conservation of bio-resources in its 26 principles. In 1993, the *Convention on Biological Diversity* came into effect, which set three objectives – the conservation of biological diversity, the sustainable use of its components, and the fair and equitable sharing of the benefits arising out of the utilization of genetic resources, ushering in a new era for the protection of global biodiversity.

China is setting up protected areas (PAs) and opening national parks on a trial basis, to create a PA framework with a focus on national parks. It was the first in the world to propose and implement the red line strategy for ecological conservation, and has designated priority areas in biodiversity conservation. These measures have contributed to the conservation of key natural ecosystems, biological resources, and habitats for key species.

Since 1956 when the first nature reserve was started, China has made nearly 10,000 PAs of different kinds and levels, covering about 18% of all its land. Recently, it has developed a PA system mainly centered on national parks. These parks are supported by nature reserves and added to by nature parks. This lays the groundwork for safeguarding natural homes, enhancing the environment, and securing the country's ecological balance. Since 2015, it has introduced 10 national parks on a trial basis, including one in Sanjiangyuan, where the Yangtze, Yellow, and Lancang rivers begin. The relevant protected areas have been merged into these national parks, managed together, and given complete protection and careful restoration.

This well-organized PA system has brought 90% of land-based ecosystem types and 71% of important wildlife species under good protection. The homes for wild animals are getting bigger, and their numbers are increasing. For example, the number of giant pandas in the wild has risen from 1,114 to 1,864 over the past four decades. The population of crested ibises has surged from only 7 to over 5,000, including both wild and artificially bred ones. The population of Asian elephants in the wild has increased from 180 in the 1980s to about 300 now. The wild population of Hainan Gibbons has grown from fewer than 10 in two groups 40 years ago to 35 in 5 groups.

 ## New Words

species	/ˈspiːʃiːz/	n.	物种
aggregate	/ˈægrɪgət/	n.	总数；合计
bearing	/ˈbeərɪŋ/	n.	关系；影响
conserve	/kənˈsɜːv/	v.	保护；保存
declaration	/ˌdeklə'reɪʃən/	n.	宣言；声明
utilization	/ˌjuːtɪlaɪˈzeɪʃən/	n.	利用；使用
genetic	/dʒɪˈnetɪk/	adj.	遗传的；基因的
priority	/praɪˈɒrɪti/	n.	优先事项；重点
habitat	/ˈhæbɪtæt/	n.	栖息地
restoration	/ˌrestəˈreɪʃən/	n.	恢复；修复

 ## Phrases and Expressions

nature reserve	自然保护区
biological diversity	生物多样性
genetic resource	遗传资源
protected area (PA)	保护区
ecological balance	生态平衡
national park	国家公园
trial basis	试验性基础
nature park	自然公园
key specie	关键物种
wild population	野生种群

Reading 2   Biodiversity Conservation Practices in Brazil

Brazil is the most biologically diverse country in the world. It is classified at the top among the world's 17 megadiverse countries, and second only to Indonesia in terms of species endemism. It contains two biodiversity hotspots (the Atlantic Forest and the Cerrado), six terrestrial biomes and three large marine ecosystems. At least 103,870 animal species and 43,020 plant species are currently known, comprising 70% of the world's catalogued animal and plant species. It is estimated that Brazil hosts between 15%-20% of the world's biological diversity, with the greatest number of endemic species on a global scale. Brazil's biodiversity is ever-expanding, with an average of 700 new animal species discovered each year.

Biodiversity is a hugely important resource, not only in terms of the environmental services it also provides in regard to the opportunities presented for development and sustainable use. Represented by more than 200 indigenous peoples and 170 languages, Brazil is megadiverse from a cultural perspective as well. This large number of local communities and villages possesses considerable knowledge on flora and fauna species, including on the traditional management systems for these natural resources. The contribution of these communities is therefore fundamental for the conservation and sustainable use of the country's genetic and biological resources.

Brazil has started several activities specifically connected to carrying out the Aichi Biodiversity Targets, including: creating ecological corridors, groups of protected areas; managing forests in a way that is good for the environment, including non-timber products; farming in a way that is good for the environment (for example, Brazil is working on a National Strategy for Supporting Combined Production in Agriculture, with the goals of supporting sustainable development and making Brazilian farming more competitive; encouraging small-scale family farming; making organic agricultural products).

Brazil is the country that made the most and largest protected areas in the world between 2006 and 2010. By the middle of 2010, 27.10% of the Brazilian Amazon area was officially protected, along with 7.33% of the Caatinga, 8.43% of the Cerrado, 8.99% of the Atlantic Forest, 4.79% of the Pantanal, 3.50% of the Pampas, and 3.14% of the Brazilian Coastal and Marine zone (including the sea and the Exclusive Economic Zone). To help protect the areas near the coast, marine, and freshwater areas and the different creatures there, Brazil has followed the practice of "defeso" since 1984. This means stopping fishing for certain targeted species during their time of reproduction. Also, the National Protected Areas Plan (PNAP) thinks about using areas where no fishing is allowed inside and outside protected areas (under SNUC) as part of a system of protected areas that represents different types of areas. Some marine protected areas that can be used sustainably are already doing this.

New Words

megadiverse	/ˌmegədaɪˈvɜːs/	adj.	生物极其多样化的
endemism	/ˈendɪmɪzəm/	n.	地方特有性；特有现象
catalogued	/ˈkætəlɒgd/	adj.	编目的；记录的
endemic	/enˈdemɪk/	adj.	特有的；地方性的
reproduction	/ˌriːprəˈdʌkʃən/	n.	繁殖；再生产

 Phrases and Expressions

terrestrial biome	陆地生物群系
indigenous peoples	原住民；土著人民
flora and fauna	动植物群
marine ecosystems	海洋生态系统
endemic species	特有物种
ecological corridors	生态廊道
non-timber products	非木材产品
Exclusive Economic Zone (EEZ)	专属经济区 (EEZ)
National Protected Areas Plan (PNAP)	国家保护区计划 (PNAP)
marine protected areas	海洋保护区

Speaking Activity: Exploring Biodiversity Conservation, High-Context Cultures and Low-Context Cultures in Intercultural Communication

Step 1: Pre-Reading and Cultural Contexts Insight

(1) Start with sharing your thoughts and knowledge on biodiversity conservation and its significance.

(2) Get familiar with high-context and low-context cultures. Understand that high-context cultures communicate in ways that are not always spoken—think gestures, silence, and the atmosphere—common in countries like China and Japan. Low-context cultures, like those in the USA and Germany, rely on clear, direct verbal communication.

(3) Consider how these cultural differences might influence working together on global issues like biodiversity conservation.

Step 2: Read and Research

(1) Form small groups and each group focuses on one of the provided texts about biodiversity conservation efforts.

(2) Look up additional examples online on how various cultures tackle biodiversity conservation.

(3) Jot down important points, especially noting how cultural contexts might shape the conservation strategies you learn about.

Step 3: Discuss Cultural Contexts in Groups

(1) With your group, talk about how the biodiversity conservation approach in your example might reflect either a high-context or low-context communication style.

(2) Create a brief presentation on your group's discoveries, focusing on the role of cultural context in conservation efforts.

Step 4: Share and Learn Through Presentations

(1) Share what your group learned about the cultural context and its influence on biodiversity conservation.

(2) Engage in a discussion about how cultural differences impact global collaboration for biodiversity conservation. Reflect on how understanding cultural contexts can lead to better communication across different cultures.

Step 5: Reflect and Role-Play

(1) With your group, devise a scenario that involves working together on a biodiversity conservation project across cultures.

(2) Act out your scenarios. After each performance, discuss as a class the communication strategies that worked well and how cultural contexts played a role.

(3) Write down your own takeaways on how cultural context awareness is crucial in intercultural communication, especially when addressing global challenges like biodiversity conservation.

PART **III** Understanding Global Issues

Directions: Discuss the following questions with your group members. Note down the key information and share your insights with the entire class.

(1) What do you think are the main threats to biodiversity, and how do human activities contribute to species loss?

(2) What are the challenges and opportunities for restoring the degraded ecosystems?

(3) How do we balance human development with the preservation of biodiversity?

(4) How can international collaboration help address global biodiversity challenges?

PART **IV** Developing Intercultural Communication Competence

Activity 1   Know the Unknown in Intercultural Communication

Directions: Read the following scenarios and discuss the key elements of intercultural communication involved. Explore why misunderstandings may arise when individuals from these different cultural backgrounds interact.

Scenario 1: Business Meetings

In a business meeting, a Japanese manager might imply that a project proposal needs more work by saying something indirect like, "This is a good start, but let's continue to develop our understanding." A colleague from America might interpret this as approval to proceed, not realizing that, in the context of Japanese communication, this is a polite way of asking for significant revisions.

Scenario 2: Feedback in the Workplace

An American supervisor provides direct, constructive feedback to an employee from China, saying, "Your report was not detailed enough; I need you to redo it with more specific data." The employee, unaccustomed to direct criticism, might feel personally offended or embarrassed, misinterpreting the feedback as dissatisfaction with their overall performance rather than a specific request for more detailed work.

Scenario 3: Email Communication

An employee from Saudi Arabia sends an email to a German colleague, filled with polite language and an update on a project, ending with, "We trust your expertise for the next steps." This subtly requests specific feedback. However, the German, used to direct requests, overlooks the implicit ask, responding with a general offer of help but without the detailed guidance expected by the Saudi colleague.

Scenario 4: Negotiation Tactics

During negotiations, a Swedish businessman gets straight to the point, outlining terms and conditions upfront. His Indian counterpart, coming from a high-context culture where building a relationship and trust is important before business dealings, might view this approach as aggressive or impersonal, potentially hindering the negotiation process.

Scenario 5: Scheduling Meetings

A Canadian manager proposes a strict agenda and clear objectives for an upcoming meeting with a Mexican team. The Mexican team, used to a more flexible approach where meetings start with informal discussions as a way to build rapport, might find the Canadian approach too rigid and impersonal, leading to a misunderstanding of the meeting's purpose and expectations.

Activity 2   Context Matters

Directions: Read the text provided below and engage in a discussion about the importance of context in cross-cultural communications.

Context significantly influences the rules and norms of communication. Depending whether the meaning is derived more from the contextual environment or the actual words spoken, communication can be defined as high-context or low-context. In high-context cultures, a lot of the message is read between the lines, through gestures, inferences, and even what is not said. On the other side, low-context cultures rely heavily on the words themselves to convey meaning, with less emphasis on nonverbal cues and the surrounding situation.

Understanding the specific situation or context in which communication occurs is essential for effective cross-cultural interaction. Context provides a framework that deeply affects the way we interact, setting the rules for appropriate behaviors, words, and ways of speaking. It is akin to the rules of a game, where each culture has developed its own set of guidelines over generations. For instance, in a business setting, the context not only includes the physical location, such as an office or a conference room, but also the cultural background of the participants, the hierarchy within the organization, and the purpose of the interaction. A meeting between people from high-context culture (e.g. Middle Eastern countries) and low-context culture (e.g. America) might need both sides to adjust. Americans often like to get straight to the point, while people from the Middle East usually focus on building a personal connection and respect for authority before talking business. Grasping the specific context in which communication occurs is a cornerstone of effective intercultural interaction. This involves a keen awareness of the cultural, social, and personal backgrounds of those we are engaging with.

PART Ⓥ Introduction to the Course Project

On-Site Shooting Plan Template for a Short Video

Creating an on-site shooting plan for short videos is essential for efficient production. This plan helps in organizing the shooting, ensuring that all necessary shots are captured, and minimizing the time spent on location. Here is a template you can use and adapt based on your specific needs:

- Project Title:
- Date:
- Location:
- Director:
- Camera Operator:
- Producer:
- Camera Operation (if applicable):
- Sound Recording (if applicable):
- Lighting Setup (if applicable):

Project Overview:

- Brief Description: (Provide a short summary of the video's purpose and content.)
- Target Audience: (Describe who the video is intended for.)
- Desired Outcome: (What do you want to achieve with this video?)

Production Day:

Arrival and Setup:

- Time: (Insert Time)

- Tasks: (List tasks such as "Set up lighting", "Test audio equipment", etc.)

Shooting Schedule:

- Scene 1: (Description)

  ✓ Location:

  ✓ Time:

  ✓ Shot Details: (List specific shots, angles, and any important notes.)

- Scene 2: (Description)

  ✓ Location: (Specific Location)

  ✓ Time: (Insert Time)

  ✓ Shot Details: (List specific shots, angles, and any important notes.)

(Repeat the format for each scene until all planned footage is captured.)

This template is a starting point. Depending on the complexity of your shooting, you may need to add or remove sections to better fit your project's needs. Always consider the specific requirements of your video, the location, and the team's capabilities when finalizing your on-site shooting plan.

Unit 5

Deforestation

Quiz 5

Learning Objectives:

After studying this unit, you should be able to

- develop a comprehensive understanding of deforestation on a global scale;

- develop awareness of cultural values to improve intercultural communication;

- apply production tips to craft a quality short video.

PART I Listening and Speaking

Section 1 Pre-Listening Activity

Direction: *Discuss the following questions with your classmates. List the key information, and prepare to share your opinion with the class.*

(1) What is your understanding of deforestation, and why do you think it's such an important issue globally?

(2) How do you think deforestation impacts local communities and people who depend on forests for their livelihoods?

(3) In your opinion, what role can governments play in addressing deforestation, and what policies do you think would be most effective?

(4) How can consumers contribute to combating deforestation through their everyday choices and purchasing habits?

(5) What are some alternative sources of income or sustainable practices that could help reduce the need for deforestation in areas where it's currently prevalent?

(6) Do you know any successful examples of reforestation or forest conservation efforts that have been implemented in recent years?

Section 2 Listening Comprehension

Passage 1

1. Directions: *Listen to Passage 1 and choose the best answer to each question.*

(1) What is one of the major threats to Australia's wildlife and ecosystems mentioned in the article?

A. Industrial pollution.

B. Climate change-induced floods.

C. Deforestation caused by human activities.

D. Invasive plant species.

(2) According to the article, how many species are at risk of extinction due to the fires?

A. At least three.

B. At least six.

C. More than ten.

D. The exact number is unknown.

(3) Which Australian state has experienced the most devastating impact from the fires, as mentioned in the passage?

A. Victoria.

B. Queensland.

C. Western Australia.

D. New South Wales.

(4) What species of bee is of particular concern due to habitat destruction caused by the fires?

A. Honeybee.

B. Bumblebee.

C. Metallic-green bee.

D. Carpenter bee.

(5) How fast is the forest equivalent to the Melbourne Cricket Ground disappearing in Australia?

A. Every 60 seconds.

B. Every 75 seconds.

C. Every 86 seconds.

D. Every 100 seconds.

Passage 2

Directions: Listen to Passage 2 and fill in the missing figures and words.

According to data released by the Ministry of Ecology and Environment at the main venue of the 2021 National Low-carbon Day, Ant Forest has attracted more than (1) _____ million people to participate in low-carbon living since its launch in (2) _____, generating over (3) _____ million tons of "green energy".

In order to encourage the low-carbon lifestyles of the general public, Ant Forest has participated in ecological restoration work in (4) _____ provinces nationwide over the past five years, planting a total of (5) _____ million trees, with over (6) _____ trees planted in Gansu and Inner Mongolia respectively. Meanwhile, Ant Forest has also established (7) _____ public welfare protection areas in ten provinces nationwide, safeguarding over (8) _____ species of wild animals and plants. Through ecological environmental protection projects across the country, Ant Forest has created a total of (9) _____ opportunities for green employment in planting, nurturing, and patrolling, bringing in a labor income of (10) _____ yuan for local residents.

PART Ⅱ Reading and Speaking

Reading 1 How China Brought Its Forests Back to Life in a Decade

Over recent decades, most countries around the world have been cutting down their trees at alarming rates. Since the 1990s, however, China has bucked this trend, achieving the most extensive reforestation of any country in the world. In 2015, forest coverage reached 22.2% of China's vast territory, up from 16.74% in 1990. This means that forests were rehabilitated over 5.5% of China's enormous landmass—511,807 square kilometres.

The key catalyst for China's rapid transition to restore forest land was a series of environmental crises caused by land degradation that struck the nation towards the end of the twentieth century. Soil erosion from the Loess Plateau was a significant contributor to the dust storms that swept through Beijing during the 1980s and 1990s. In 1997, severe droughts saw the lower reaches of the Yellow River dry up for 267 days, putting at severe risk the availability of water around the northern plains. Just a year later, devastating flooding occurred along the Yangtze River. With a view to avert further such crises in the future, in 1999, the Chinese government launched the "Grain for Green" program.

What is extraordinary about that the transformation of China's depleted landscapes is that it was achieved through the mass participation of tens of millions of Chinese people. The "Grain for Green" program directly compensated farmers for restoring and protecting forests and natural vegetation where they had formerly planted crops or herded livestock.

Initially, farmers were compensated for their labour in a massive engineering project that extended across much of China's rural landscape—digging reservoirs at the bottom of valleys and terraces into the hillsides, to help the land to retain water and resist erosion. They were instructed to keep their animals penned up to prevent damage to the newly restored land through over-grazing of livestock. On the reconstructed landscape they planted natural vegetation and trees in designated areas, and were also assigned plots to develop their own crops. Farmers were granted land rights to the fields and terraces they maintained and control over their produce, as well as subsidies for protecting the newly planted forests.

The Chinese experience is highly significant for the future of degraded landscapes around the world. The global population boom and massive expansion of agriculture since the 1950s means that soil degradation and desertification is a growing problem in most arid and semi-arid landscapes of the Global South, which is likely to be worsened with the impacts of climate change. Indeed, the transferability of lessons from China's forestry programmes has already been proven—the methods piloted in China to rehabilitate land that had been degraded over millennia have since been replicated in Sub-Saharan Africa with initial successes in Rwanda and Ethiopia.

 New Words

reforestation	/ˌriːfɒrɪ'steɪʃən/	n.	再造林；重新造林
rehabilitate	/ˌriːə'bɪlɪteɪt/	v.	恢复；修复
landmass	/'lænd͵mæs/	n.	陆地；大陆
degradation	/degrə'deɪʃən/	n.	退化
erosion	/ɪ'rəʊʒən/	n.	流失；腐蚀
drought	/draʊt/	n.	干旱
flooding	/'flʌdɪŋ/	n.	洪水；泛滥
avert	/ə'vɜːt/	v.	避免；防止
depleted	/dɪ'pliːtɪd/	adj.	耗尽的；贫乏的
compensate	/'kɒmpenseɪt/	v.	补偿；赔偿
livestock	/'laɪvstɒk/	n.	牲畜；家畜
reservoir	/'rezəvwɑː/	n.	水库；蓄水池
terrace	/'terəs/	n.	梯田；平台
over-grazing	/'əʊvə 'greɪzɪŋ/	n.	过度放牧
subsidy	/'sʌbsɪdi/	n.	补贴；津贴
desertification	/dɪˌzɜːtɪfɪ'keɪʃən/	n.	沙漠化
transferability	/ˌtrænsfərə'bɪlɪti/	n.	可转移性；可转让性

 Phrases and Expressions

| forest cover | 森林覆盖率 |

land degradation	土地退化
soil erosion	水土流失
dust storm	沙尘暴
grain for green	退耕还林
land rights	土地权利
degraded landscape	退化的景观
Global South	全球南方

Reading 2   We're Off Track to Protect and Restore Forests by 2030

WWF's Forest Pathways 2023 report and the Forest Declaration Assessment detail the immense scale of forest loss just two years after more than 130 countries representing 85% of the planet's forests pledged to halt and reverse deforestation by the end of the decade. The lack of progress on commitments leaves the world in clear danger of missing vital targets.

In 2022, global deforestation reached 16.3 million acres, with primary tropical forest loss at 10.1 million acres. Alarmingly, 96% of deforestation takes place in tropical regions. Tropical Asia is the only region close to achieving zero deforestation. Without urgent action, tropical forests will begin to act as a carbon source, not a sink, under the pressures of a warming, drying, and increasingly extreme climate. Widespread and increasing deforestation and degradation in the planet's three largest tropical forest basins—the Amazon, Congo, and the forests of Asia-Pacific—could deliver a global climate catastrophe.

Fortunately, there's still time to halt deforestation and sustainably manage and restore forests in ways that benefit people and nature. "If we're serious about ensuring a future for forests—and halting the biodiversity and climate crises—time is of the essence," said Kerry Cesareo, senior vice president for forests at WWF. "While the numbers are stark, we know what we need to do. And the Forest Pathways report provides tangible guidance for decision-makers, from governments to financial institutions to private sector actors."

Globally, at least 100 times more public funding goes to environmentally harmful subsidies than financing to help forests. Only $2.2 billion in public funds is channeled to forests each year—a mere fraction compared to other global investments. Indigenous peoples and local communities do not receive the necessary resources to secure their rights and effectively manage their lands, even though tropical forests under their stewardship are better protected and deforestation and degradation are lower.

Forest Pathways outlines specific steps countries can take to save forests. In addition to calling for governments to meet their financial promises, the report sets out a blueprint to save forests by 2030, with essential measures, including:

- Ending forest-harming investments and subsidies such as agricultural subsidies responsible for the loss of 5.4 million acres of forest per year;

- Reforming the rules of global trade that harm forests, cutting deforesting commodities out of global supply chains, and removing barriers to forest-friendly goods;

- Accelerating the recognition of land rights to indigenous peoples;

- Making the shift toward nature-based economies.

New Words

halt	/hɔːlt/	v.	停止；阻止
deforestation	/ˌdiːfɒrɪ'steɪʃən/	n.	森林砍伐；毁林
commitment	/kə'mɪtmənt/	n.	承诺；责任
primary	/'praɪməri/	adj.	主要的，首要的，原始的
tropical	/'trɒpɪkəl/	adj.	热带的，热带地区的
degradation	/ˌdegrə'deɪʃən/	n.	退化；恶化
catastrophe	/'kə'tæstrəfi/	n.	灾难
tangible	/'tændʒəbl/	adj.	有形的；具体的
stewardship	/'stjuːədʃɪp/	n.	管理；保护
commodity	/kə'mɒdɪti/	n.	商品；货物
recognition	/ˌrekəg'nɪʃən/	n.	认可；承认

Phrases and Expressions

forest pathways report	森林路径报告
forest loss	森林损失
global deforestation	全球森林砍伐
carbon source	碳源
tropical forest basin	热带森林盆地
environmentally harmful subsidy	对环境有害的补贴

| supply chain | 供应链 |
| nature-based economy | 基于自然的经济 |

Speaking Activity: Exploring Deforestation and Cultural Perspectives

Step 1: Reading and Comprehension

(1) Each group will be assigned one of the two reading passages.

(2) Read your assigned passage individually and highlight key information about reforestation efforts or deforestation challenges in China or globally.

(3) In your group, discuss the main points of your passage and clarify any questions you have.

Step 2: Jigsaw Activity

(1) You will be rearranged into new groups, ensuring that each new group has members who have read both passages.

(2) Take turns to share the key information from your original passage with your new group members.

(3) Ask questions and discuss the similarities and differences between the two passages.

Step 3: Learning About Kluckhohn and Strodtbeck's Man-Nature Orientation

(1) Research on Kluckhohn and Strodtbeck's Man-Nature Orientation, explaining the three categories: subjugation to nature, harmony with nature, and mastery over nature.

(2) Find examples of how different cultures might view their relationship with nature based on this orientation.

Step 4: Applying Man-Nature Orientation to Deforestation

(1) In your groups, discuss how different Man-Nature Orientations might influence a culture's approach to deforestation and reforestation efforts.

(2) Consider the following questions:

- How might a culture view itself as subjugated to nature approach to deforestation and reforestation? What about a culture that seeks harmony with nature or one that believes in mastery over nature?

● How might these orientations impact the success of reforestation efforts, as seen in the passages about China and global efforts?

(3) Prepare a short summary of your group's discussion.

Step 5: Group Presentations and Class Discussion

(1) Present your summary to the class, highlighting the potential impact of Man-Nature Orientation on deforestation and reforestation efforts.

(2) After all groups have presented, participate in a class discussion on the following questions:

● How might understanding different Man-Nature Orientations help in addressing global deforestation challenges?

● What can we learn from the successful reforestation efforts in China, and how might these lessons be applied in other countries with different cultural perspectives?

PART **III** Understanding Global Issues

Directions: *Discuss the following questions with your group members. Note down the key information and share your insights with the entire class.*

(1) In your opinion, what are the environmental consequences of deforestation?

(2) What are the economic benefits and drawbacks of deforestation?

(3) How can international cooperation and partnerships help address global deforestation?

(4) How can individuals contribute to efforts to combat deforestation in their daily lives?

PART **IV** Developing Intercultural Communication Competence

Activity 1   Value the Values in Intercultural Communication

Directions: *Read the following scenarios and discuss the key cultural values involved in intercultural communication. Explore why misunderstandings may arise when individuals from different cultural backgrounds interact.*

Scenario 1: Who Goes First?

Liam, a Chinese PhD student on an academic exchange in Canada, visits Dr. Richardson, a senior professor, for a research discussion. As they reach the office door, Dr. Richardson opens it and gestures for Liam to go in first. She hesitates for a moment but then steps inside, feeling a bit unsure. Back in China, the roles would be reversed. In a similar situation, Liam would be the one hurrying to open the door for her professor as a sign of respect. The professor, in turn, would pause and wait for her to hold it fully before walking in.

Scenario 2: Dams vs. Rivers

A team are working on saving an endangered area. Part of the team is from the Netherlands, known for building things like dams to control water and protect land. The other part of the team comes from Native American communities, who believe in living in harmony with nature rather than changing it. The Dutch suggest building new dams to stop flooding, showing their approach to fix nature problems with technology. The Native Americans recommend using natural ways to deal with the water, like restoring old river paths, believing this respects nature's own systems.

Activity 2　Developing Cultural Value Awareness

Directions: *Read the text below and engage in a discussion regarding the contents in Table 5.1 and Table 5.2.*

Cultural value awareness refers to the recognition, understanding, and appreciation of the diverse values, beliefs, norms, and practices that characterize different cultures. It involves an acknowledgment of the deep-seated cultural forces that influence individuals' worldviews, behaviors, and communication styles. Developing cultural value awareness is a crucial step in cultivating intercultural competence, which is the ability to communicate effectively and appropriately with people from other cultures. Cultural value awareness is closely linked to several intercultural communication (IC) theories and concepts. Here are two IC theories and concepts related to cultural value awareness:

(1) Hofstede's Cultural Dimensions Theory: This theory identifies six dimensions along which cultures can be analyzed and compared: Power Distance, Individualism vs. Collectivism, Masculinity vs. Femininity, Uncertainty Avoidance, Long-Term vs. Short-Term Orientation, and Indulgence vs. Restraint.

Table 5.1   Hofstede's Cultural Dimensions

Dimension	Description
Power Distance	The dimension deals with the extent to which a society accepts equal of unequal distribution of power in its relationships, institutions, and organizations.
Individualism vs. Collectivism	This dimension examines the degree to which a society endorses individuals' independence or prioritizes the group's cohesion and interdependence.
Masculinity vs. Femininity	The preference of a society for achievement, heroism, and material success (masculinity) versus cooperation, modesty, and quality of life (femininity).
Uncertainty Avoidance	This assesses a culture's tolerance for ambiguity and its need for established norms and rules to minimize uncertainty.
Long-Term vs. Short-Term Orientation	It captures whether a culture values long-term commitments and future rewards over short-term gains and immediate outcomes.
Indulgence vs. Restraint	The extent to which a society allows free gratification of basic human desires related to enjoying life and having fun (indulgence) compared to suppressing gratification by means of strict social norms (restraint).

(2) **Kluckhohn and Strodtbeck's Value Orientations**: Kluckhohn and Strodtbeck's framework is an important anthropological model that identifies how cultures differ based on their responses to five universal life questions (Human nature orientation, Man-nature orientation, Time orientation, Activity orientation, and Relational orientation). Here's a more detailed look at each of the five orientations they proposed:

Table 5.2   Kluckhohn and Strodtbeck's Value Orientations

Orientation	Value and Behavior Range		
Human nature	Basically evil	Mixture of good and evil	Basically good
Humans and nature	Subject to nature	Harmony with nature	Master of nature
Sense of time	Past	Present	Future
Activity	Being	Being-in-becoming	Doing
Social relationships	Authoritarian	Group	Individualism

PART Ⅴ Introduction to the Course Project

Production Tips for Creating a Short Video

Creating a short video can be an exciting project, but it's important to approach the production phase with attention to detail to ensure a smooth process and high-quality outcome. Here are some key considerations to guide you through the production of the short video:

- **Check Equipment Before Shooting:** Ensure all of your equipment, including cameras, microphones, and lights, are in working order. Charge the batteries and have backups ready.

- **Lighting:** Good lighting is crucial for video quality. Shoot in well-lit areas or use additional lighting equipment to eliminate shadows and enhance visual clarity.

- **Audio Quality:** Clear audio is as important as video quality. Use external microphones if possible and monitor audio levels during recording. Avoid noisy locations and wind interference.

- **Framing and Composition**: Pay attention to how each shot is framed. Use the rule of thirds for a balanced composition and adjust the camera angle and position to best capture the scene.

- **Keep Shots Stable:** Use tripods or stabilizers to keep your camera steady. Shaky footage can distract viewers and detract from the video's quality.

- **Follow the Shooting Plan**: Stick to your storyboard or shooting plan, but also be flexible if you find opportunities for improvements or need to adapt to unforeseen circumstances.

- **Capture B-Roll:** Shoot extra footage of the environment, objects, or additional angles of the main action. B-Roll is essential for editing, providing cutaways and context to your story.

- **Monitor Continuity:** Ensure that the visual aspects of your shots remain consistent, especially when shooting scenes out of sequence. Pay attention to details like lighting, props, and actors' positions.

- **Perform Multiple Takes:** Do not rely on a single take for each scene. Shooting multiple takes gives you options during editing, ensuring you have the best possible version of each scene.

- **Safety First:** Always prioritize the safety of the team members. Follow safety guidelines, especially when using props, or shooting in challenging locations.

- **Communication:** Keep open and clear communication among all team members. Collaboration and adaptability are key to addressing challenges and making on-the-spot decisions.

- **Backup Footage Regularly:** Regularly back up your footage to avoid data loss. It's advisable to have multiple copies in different locations.

By keeping these points in mind, you can navigate the production phase more effectively, leading to a successful and rewarding video project. Remember, the goal is not just to complete an assignment but to tell a compelling story through your video.

Unit 6

Natural Disasters

Quiz 6

Learning Objectives:

After studying this unit, you should be able to

● develop a comprehensive understanding of natural disasters on a global scale;

● understand and apply key elements of the Process Model of Intercultural communication;

● apply post-production techniques to enhance the short video.

PART **I** Listening and Speaking

Section 1 Pre-Listening Activity

Directions: Discuss the following questions with your classmates. List the key information, and prepare to share your opinion with the class.

(1) How would you define a natural disaster, and what are some examples you can think of?

(2) Have you ever experienced a severe thunderstorm or hailstorm? How did it affect you or your surroundings?

(3) Have you encountered any extreme heatwaves or cold spells in your area? How did people cope with them?

(4) In what ways do natural disasters affect communities, both in the short term and the long term?

(5) How important are education and raising public awareness in reducing vulnerability to natural disasters? What initiatives can be implemented to enhance public understanding and preparedness?

(6) How can technology, such as early warning systems or remote sensing, help in predicting and mitigating the effects of natural disasters?

Section 2 Listening Comprehension

Passage 1

1. Directions: Listen to Passage 1 and choose the best answer to each question.

(1) What does the term "natural disasters" refer to?

A. Human-made phenomena.

B. Events that benefit human survival.

C. Weather forecasts.

D. Natural phenomena harmful to human survival.

(2) According to the passage, which type of natural disaster is the most frequent?

A. Geological disasters.

B. Oceanic disasters.

C. Biological disasters.

D. Meteorological disasters.

(3) What did Celeste Saulo express concerns about in the report findings?

A. Rising global temperatures.

B. Decreasing storm frequency.

C. Record heatwaves in Asia.

D. Decreasing economic losses.

(4) How fast is Asia warming compared to the global average since the 1960–1990 period?

A. Three times faster.

B. Half as fast.

C. Twice as fast.

D. Not mentioned in the article.

(5) What region experienced severe dust storms, lightning, and thick smog in 2023?

A. North America.   B. Asia.

C. Europe.   D. Africa.

2. Directions: *Listen to Passage 1 again and decide whether the statements are true (T) or false (F).*

(6) _____ Meteorological disasters include earthquakes and landslides.

(7) _____ Asia faced severe dust storms and thick smog in 2023.

(8) _____ Celeste Saulo expressed satisfaction with the report findings.

(9) _____ Asia experienced below-normal precipitation levels overall in 2023.

(10) _____ Sea-surface temperatures in the Arctic Ocean reached record highs in 2023.

Passage 2

1. Directions: *Listen to Passage 2 and choose the best answer to each question.*

(1) What are natural hazards?

    A. Events with social origins.

    B. Rapid or slow physical phenomena.

    C. Human-made disasters.

    D. Environmental changes.

(2) What is disaster risk reduction?

    A. Increasing disaster risks.

    B. Ignoring causal factors of disasters.

    C. Analyzing and reducing disaster risks systematically.

    D. Enhancing vulnerability.

(3) What is UNESCO's role in disaster risk reduction?

    A. Promoting risk awareness, prevention, and preparedness.

    B. Advocating for increased vulnerability.

    C. Encouraging disaster occurrence.

    D. Supporting risk ignorance.

(4) What topics does UNESCO support Member States on?

    A. Disaster celebration.

    B. Environment destruction.

    C. Science, technology, and innovation for resilience.

    D. Promoting vulnerability.

(5) How does UNESCO implement its disaster risk reduction work?

    A. Through increasing vulnerability.

B. By ignoring social sciences.

C. By collaborating with governments, civil society, and other organizations.

D. By promoting risk acceptance.

2. Directions: Answer the following three questions based on the information you hear.

(6) What is Disaster Risk Reduction (DRR) and why is it important?

_____

_____

(7) How does UNESCO contribute to DRR?

_____

_____

(8) What are some of the key areas in which UNESCO supports Member States regarding DRR?

_____

_____

PART Ⅱ Reading and Speaking

Reading 1　China's National Demonstration Communities for Disaster Risk Reduction

Building resilient communities can mitigate natural disaster risks. Since the concept of a disaster-resistant community was first proposed in the United States in 1994, Community-Based Disaster Risk Reduction (CBDRR) has been seen worldwide as a crucial approach to effectively improve disaster response capabilities, mitigating disaster losses and risks.

The most basic administrative unit in China, communities (or "villages" as they are called in rural areas), have played an increasingly important role in the country's comprehensive DRR efforts in the 21st century. Underscoring China's commitment to community-based disaster risk management, in 2007, the National Commission for Disaster Reduction of China began to implement a nationwide project to designate selected communities as demonstration communities for DRR. The goal is to promote and encourage capacity building on DRR in the surrounding vicinity, in large part by strengthening awareness about DRR.

Under the project, which is called the National Demonstration Communities on DRR, communities can apply to their respective provincial departments of civil affairs to become a Comprehensive Disaster Reduction Demonstration Community. The **evaluation** of the application covers three main components: infrastructure, community residents' capacity, and disaster management. If the application is successful, the community is subjected to a standardized evaluation of its DRR capacity building efforts. All communities across China are encouraged to **mobilize** all possible resources from all types of **stakeholders** (e.g., various level of governments, industries, academia, volunteers) to facilitate DRR capacity building.

The number of DRR demonstration communities in every province in China has risen dramatically over the last decade, especially since 2011. By the end of 2018, the total number of these communities had exceeded 12,535, nearly 40 times higher than in 2008. By the end of 2017, DRR demonstration communities had achieved 100% coverage at the provincial level and 87% coverage at the county and city level. Counties and cities in the capital circle, the Yangtze River Delta and the Pearl River Delta account for over a third (35%) of the total number of DRR demonstration communities in China.

Much of the growth in the number of demonstration communities has been driven by goal setting in national plans and policies. In November 2011, the General Office of the State Council issued the National Comprehensive Disaster Prevention and Mitigation Plan (2011–2015), which set the goal of creating 5,000 national comprehensive disaster reduction demonstration communities, in line with the broader aim of strengthening **grassroots** disaster prevention and mitigation capacity building in both rural and urban areas. The National Comprehensive Disaster Prevention and Mitigation Plan of the 13th Five-Year (2016–2020), issued by the General Office of the State Council, set the goal of adding 5,000 more demonstration communities during this five-year period.

New Words

resilient	/rɪ'zɪliənt/	*adj.*	有弹性的；能迅速恢复的
disaster-resistant	/dɪ'zɑːstə rɪ'zɪstənt/	*adj.*	抗灾的；防灾的
capacity	/kə'pæsɪti/	*n.*	能力；容量

evaluation	/ɪˌvæljʊˈeɪʃən/	n.	评估；评价
mobilize	/ˈməʊbɪlaɪz/	v.	动员；调动
stakeholder	/ˈsteɪkˌhəʊldə/	n.	利益相关者；股东
grassroots	/ˈɡrɑːsˌruːts/	n.	基层；草根

 ## Phrases and Expressions

Disaster Risk Reduction (DRR)	降低灾害风险
resilient communities	有韧性的社区
capacity building	能力建设
provincial departments of civil affair	省民政部门
comprehensive disaster reduction	降低综合灾害
grassroots disaster prevention	基层灾害预防
urban and rural area	城乡地区

Reading 2   Japan Spent Decades Making Itself Earthquake Resilient

Japan is one of the most **seismically** active nations in the world. Its location between four **tectonic plates** meaning that earthquakes are a matter of when, not if. Though they often go undetected by the people walking above them, **seismic tremors** are a daily occurrence in the country, which the EarthScope Consortium reports experiences around 1,500 noticeable earthquakes each year. Given this risk, finding ways to live with earthquakes is woven into the physical and social makeup of Japanese communities.

Understanding how to best prepare for major earthquakes is often hard-won, stemming from knowledge gleaned from past disasters, says Keith Porter, chief engineer for Canada's Institute for Catastrophic Loss Reduction. In Japan, seismic **regulations** for building **codes** were first introduced after a magnitude-7.9 earthquake in 1923 killed more than 140,000 people and reduced hundreds of thousands of structures to **rubble**. These early regulations were focused on strengthening new structures being built in urban areas, adding oversight to the construction of wood and concrete buildings.

The seismic code has undergone a number of significant changes in the decades since, most notably through the Building Standard Law of 1950 and the New Earthquake Resistant Building Standards Amendment in 1981. Along with providing construction specifics, these pieces of legislation established expectations for how buildings are expected to perform during earthquakes. The 1950 Act established a standard in which buildings were expected to withstand earthquakes up to a magnitude-7 without serious issue. The 1981 Amendment gets a bit more specific with what that damage can be, stating that when earthquakes up to a magnitude-7 strike, a building should only sustain minor damage but still function as usual.

There are a number of different techniques that achieve these standards in Japan, with the choice of which to use often depending on the type of structure—such as a skyscraper or single-family home—and the budget available, along with other considerations. At a base level, buildings are fortified with thicker beams, pillars, and walls to better withstand shaking.

There are also techniques to help separate buildings from the movement of a shaking ground. One popular method is installing pads made of absorbent material like rubber at the base of a building's foundation, dampening the shock of movement to the structure itself. Another approach, the base isolation system, calls for not just having these pads at the base, but building the entire structure atop thick padding so that there is a full layer of separation between the unit and the moving earth.

Porter notes that many older Japanese buildings are traditional post and beam wood frame construction, which "tends to be very fragile" and vulnerable to earthquake damage. Following another deadly earthquake in 1995, Japan began focusing on retrofitting older architecture to be more resilient to earthquakes.

🖉 New Words

regulation	/ˌreɡjʊˈleɪʃən/	n.	规定；规则
code	/kəʊd/	n.	密码；规范
rubble	/ˈrʌbəl/	n.	瓦砾；碎石
amendment	/əˈmendmənt/	n.	修正案；改进
legislation	/ˌledʒɪsˈleɪʃən/	n.	法规；法律
withstand	/wɪðˈstænd/	v.	承受；抵挡
fortify	/ˈfɔːtɪfaɪ/	v.	加固；强化

foundation	/faʊnˈdeɪʃən/	n.	地基；基础
fragile	/ˈfrædʒaɪl/	adj.	脆弱的；易碎的
retrofit	/ˈretrəʊˌfɪt/	v.	改造；翻新

 Phrases and Expressions

tectonic plate	构造板块
seismic tremor	地震波；震动
absorbent material	吸收材料
earthquake resilience	抗震韧性
seismically active	地震活跃
building code	建筑规范
seismic regulation	抗震规定
New Earthquake Resistant Building Standards Amendment	新抗震建筑标准修正案
base isolation system	基础隔震系统
post and beam wood frame construction	柱梁木框架结构
retrofitting older architecture	改造老旧建筑
shock of movement	震动冲击

Speaking Activity: Exploring Intercultural Perspectives on Natural Disaster Preparedness

Step 1: Familiarize Yourself with the Intercultural Competence Model

(1) Read the provided handout on the Intercultural Competence Model, which includes the following components: knowledge, attitudes, skills.

(2) Discuss with your group members to ensure everyone understands the model and its relevance to intercultural communication.

Step 2: Jigsaw Activity

(1) Divide your group into two subgroups: A and B.

(2) Group A reads Text A, while Group B reads Text B.

(3) After reading, each subgroup discusses the main points and key information from their respective texts.

Step 3: Information Sharing and Comparison

(1) Regroup with your original group members.

(2) Take turns sharing the main points and key information from the texts you read.

(3) Compare and contrast the approaches to natural disaster preparedness in Japan and China, considering factors such as history, infrastructure, community involvement, and policies.

Step 4: Applying the Intercultural Competence Model (see the model in PART IV)

(1) Reflect on how the Intercultural Competence Model relates to the topic of natural disaster preparedness in Japan and China.

(2) Consider the following questions:

- Knowledge: What have you learned about the cultural contexts and practices related to disaster preparedness in Japan and China?

- Attitudes: How might cultural attitudes and values shape each country's approach to disaster preparedness?

- Skills: What communication skills are essential for effective intercultural dialogue on this topic?

(3) Share your thoughts and insights with your group members.

Step 5: Reflection and Discussion

(1) As a group, discuss the following questions:

- What lessons can be learned from China and Japan's experiences that could be applied to other countries or contexts?

- How can individuals and communities develop intercultural competence to better address global challenges like natural disasters?

(2) Summarize your group's key takeaways and be prepared to share them with the class.

PART **III** Understanding Global Issues

Directions: Discuss the following questions with your group members. Note down the key information and share your insights with the entire class.

(1) In your view, how do natural disasters impact local communities both in terms of immediate effects and long-term consequences?

(2) How does the aftermath of a natural disaster impact both physical and mental health of individuals within affected communities?

(3) What role can interdisciplinary approaches play in addressing the complex challenges posed by natural disasters?

(4) What lessons can we learn from past natural disasters and how can we apply them to improve strategies for future disaster preparedness?

PART **IV** Developing Intercultural Communication Competence

Activity 1   Addressing Intercultural Communication Challenges

Directions: In your groups, imagine each member is going to study abroad in a different country or work in a different international corporation or organization. First, brainstorm solutions for the following intercultural communication challenges. Then, summarize your proposed solutions and reflect on how developing intercultural competence enhances effectiveness in diverse settings.

Studying abroad or working internationally presents several intercultural communication challenges. Language barriers can lead to misunderstandings, while cultural differences in norms, values, and practices may cause conflicts. Stereotyping and prejudices can negatively impact interactions, and variations in nonverbal communication, such as gestures and facial expressions, can cause confusion. Adapting to different communication styles, whether direct or indirect, can be challenging. Additionally, integrating socially and building relationships within a new community or workplace culture can be difficult. Managing the stress of adjusting to a new cultural environment while maintaining effective communication adds another layer of complexity. Overcoming these obstacles involves developing intercultural competence, being open to learning, and actively engaging with diverse cultures.

Activity 2　The Process Model of Intercultural Competence

Directions: *Discuss your understanding of the elements involved in the Process Model of Intercultural Communication.*

The Process Model of Intercultural Competence, created by Dr. Darla K. Deardorff, is a dynamic framework that emphasizes the development of intercultural skills through continuous engagement and reflection. It begins with key attitudes—respect, openness, and curiosity—that lead to the acquisition of cultural knowledge and comprehension, including self-awareness and sociolinguistic understanding. By cultivating skills such as listening, observing, and evaluating, individuals can achieve internal outcomes like adaptability and empathy. This process results in effective and appropriate communication and behavior in intercultural situations, fostering successful interactions across diverse cultural contexts.

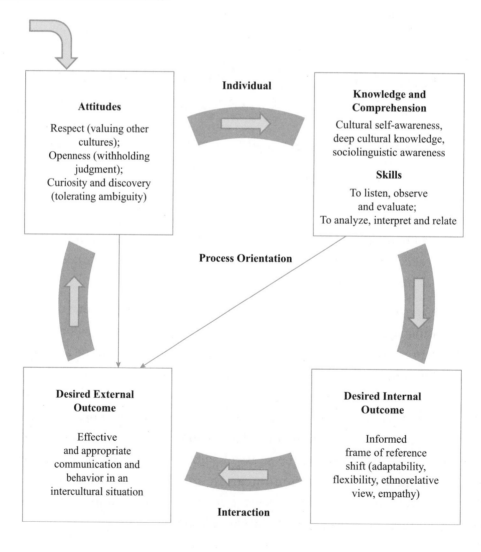

PART Ⅴ Introduction to the Course Project

Post-Production Tips for Creating a Short Video

Post-production is a crucial phase in video creation where raw footage is transformed into a polished, engaging final product. This phase involves various steps, including organizing footage, editing, enhancing audio, adding visual effects, and ensuring the overall quality of the video. Here are some essential tips to help you navigate the post-production process effectively and create a high-quality short video.

Organize Your Footage

- Review and Sort Clips: Import all your footage into your editing software and organize it into folders or bins. Label and categorize clips by scenes or types.

Editing

- Assemble Rough Cut: Start with a rough cut by placing clips in the timeline according to your script or storyboard. Focus on getting the sequence right.

- Trim and Refine: Cut out unnecessary parts and refine the transitions between clips to ensure a smooth flow.

- Pacing: Adjust the pacing to maintain viewer interest, balancing between fast cuts and slower, more reflective moments.

Audio

- Clean Up Audio: Use audio editing tools to remove background noise and enhance dialogue clarity.

- Add Background Music: Choose music that complements the mood of your video. Ensure it doesn't overpower the dialogue.

- Sound Effects: Add sound effects to enhance realism and engagement.

Visual Enhancements

- Color Correction: Adjust the color balance to ensure consistent lighting and mood across all clips.

- Color Grading: Apply a color grade to give your video a specific look or feel, enhancing the overall aesthetic.

Graphics and Titles

- Intro and Outro: Create engaging opening and closing titles. Include relevant information like the video title, credits, and any necessary disclaimers.

- Lower Thirds: Use lower thirds to introduce speakers or provide additional information without distracting from the main content.

- Subtitles: Add subtitles for accessibility and to aid understanding, especially if the audio quality isn't perfect.

Review and Feedback

- Watch Multiple Times: Review your video multiple times to catch any errors or inconsistencies.

- Feedback: Share a draft with classmates, instructors, or peers to get constructive feedback and make necessary adjustments.

Unit **7**

Recycling

Quiz 7

Learning Objectives:

After studying this unit, you should be able to

- develop a comprehensive understanding of recycling on a global scale;

- analyze the causes of intercultural miscommunication in films;;

- apply quality control and final review techniques to polish your short video.

PART I Listening and Speaking

Section 1 Pre-Listening Activity

Directions: *Discuss the following questions with your classmates. List the key information, and prepare to share your opinion with the class.*

(1) What are the benefits of recycling for the environment and society?

(2) Can you describe the recycling process for common materials like paper, plastic, and glass?

(3) What challenges do people face when trying to recycle in your community?

(4) In what ways can individuals contribute to improving recycling rates?

(5) How does recycling impact energy consumption and resource conservation?

(6) Can you suggest innovative ways or technologies that could enhance the recycling process?

Section 2 Listening Comprehension

Passage 1

1. *Directions:* *Listen to Passage 1 and choose the best answer to each question.*

(1) Why does Yang find the recycling service convenient?

    A. It offers discounts on new clothes.

    B. It allows her to recycle clothes during the day.

    C. It picks up clothes directly from her door at a scheduled time.

D. It pays her a large amount of money for her old clothes.

(2) What happens to the clothes that are relatively new or fairly used?

A. They are recycled into new raw materials.

B. They are donated to rural areas.

C. They are sold to renewable resource companies.

D. They are sent to power plants as fuel.

(3) What percentage of China's textile waste is currently recycled and reused?

A. Less than 10%.

B. About 20%.

C. More than 50%.

D. Almost all of it.

(4) What is done to the clothes that cannot be donated or treated by the recycling company?

A. They are thrown away.

B. They are stored in warehouses.

C. They are sent to power plants to be used as fuel.

D. They are exported to other countries.

(5) What are some items made from recycled light-colored fabrics?

A. Insulation materials.

B. Carpets and gloves.

C. New clothing.

D. Plastic products.

2. Directions: *Based on information from Passage 1, fill in the following blanks.*

(6) Yang loves to shop, but her problem is _____.

(7) After reading up on recycling, she tried a service through a mini program on _____.

(8) The company that runs the recycling platform says they can get up to _____ orders in a day.

(9) Clothes that are relatively new or fairly used are donated to _____ areas.

(10) Damage or older clothes are sold to _____ resource companies.

Passage 2

*2. **Directions:** Listen to Passage 2 and fill in the missing words.*

Last year, the world made a record of 53.6 million tons of (1) _____ waste. This is more than the weight of all the adults in Europe, said a report in June 2020. Asian countries threw away the most (2) _____, about 24.9 million tons. Next were the Americas with 13.1 million tons and Europe with 12 million tons. Africa and Oceania only threw away 2.9 million tons and 0.7 million tons. But the amount of e-waste per person has changed how people around the world use electronic (3) _____. Europeans throw away the most per person, about 16.2 kg each. In the Americas, it is 13.3 kg per person. In Asia and Africa, it is only 5.6 kg and 2.5 kg per person.

In the past five years, global e-waste has increased by 21%. If this continues, by 2030, the world will make over 74 million tons of e-waste. This increase is because people use many electronic goods that have short lives and are hard to repair, said the UN's Global E-waste Monitor 2020.

"We need to work much harder to make sure that electronics are made, used, and thrown away in smarter and more (4) _____ ways", said David M. Malone, a UN official. Last year, only 9.3 million tons or 18% of e-waste was collected and (5) _____. The rest, which contains valuable metals like gold, silver, copper, and platinum worth $57 billion, stayed in landfills or garbage cans. Dumping e-waste this way (6) _____ toxic and chemical waste, causing serious health problems. About 50 tons of mercury, used in monitors, light bulbs, and other equipment, leaked into the environment, harming human neurological systems. In low-income countries, informal e-waste collectors face serious health risks. They use hammers and burn electronic parts to extract valuable metals, releasing toxic fumes that can cause deadly diseases.

"More electronic waste is produced than is being safely recycled in most parts of the world," said Nikhil Seth, director of the United Nations Institute for Training and Research. "We need more cooperation to raise (7) _____ of this growing problem and take measures supported by research and training", he added.

Many countries have created national policies for collecting and recycling e-waste, increasing from 61 to 78 countries. But many still struggle to enforce these rules. Many countries have adopted extended producer responsibility (EPR), requiring

(8) _____ to collect and recycle products after consumers are done with them. But many governments still find it hard to (9) _____ these laws.

The report also raised concerns about recycling air conditioners and refrigerators. The use of these appliances has greatly increased in developing countries. Some of these machines use refrigerants that cause global warming, making their disposal a major concern. "A total of 98 million tons of CO_2 equivalents were released into the atmosphere from (10) _____ fridges and air conditioners that were not disposed of properly", said the report.

PART II Reading and Speaking

Reading 1　How Does China Handle Retired NEV Batteries?

As the adoption of New Energy Vehicles (NEVs) continues to rise, China is facing a significant increase in retired lithium batteries. Last year, China retired more than 580,000 tons of lithium batteries. The number is expected to reach 800,000 tons next year.

This surge has raised critical questions about the handling of these batteries. According to China's national standards for NEVs, when the capacity of lithium batteries falls below 80% of the rated capacity, they are no longer suitable for electric vehicles and must be recycled by qualified enterprises.

Electric car batteries weigh hundreds of kilograms. Experts say that when a vehicle is scrapped, the lithium hexafluorophosphate in the battery gets easily hydrolyzed in the air and produces harmful substances such as phosphorus pentafluoride and hydrogen fluoride, which will cause environmental pollution if not treated properly.

In addition, retired lithium batteries actually have a high use value. At present, there are two modes of lithium battery recycling: cascade utilization and material recovery. Cascade utilization involves repurposing batteries for applications with lower energy density requirements, such as energy storage systems. Material recovery focuses on extracting valuable metals like cobalt, nickel and lithium for reuse in new batteries.

The proper handling and recycling of retired lithium batteries not only mitigates environmental risks but also presents economic opportunities. By efficiently recovering valuable materials, the recycling industry can help reduce the demand for virgin resources and contribute to a more sustainable and circular economy.

With the continuous growth of China's NEV industry, the battery recycling industry has also been growing rapidly. Zhang Ying, president of the Automotive Recycling Industry Development Committee of the China Association for Economic Development in Asia, told China Media Group that there are more than 15,000 recycling **outlets** in China, which can cover more than 85% of the entire market field of NEVs.

According to the China Resources Recycling Association, in 2023, the net increase of vehicle scrap was 7.56 million, a year-on-year increase of 32%, and the standard recycling and utilization of used household appliances was about 93 million units, with a weight of about 4.4 million tons. More than 200 million pieces of furniture were recycled. Among them, the recycling and utilization of 10 major renewable resources, including scrap steel, scrap **non-ferrous metals** and waste plastics, amounted to about 392 million tons, which continued to play a prominent role in supporting national resource security.

 ## New Words

retired	/rɪˈtaɪəd/	adj.	退役的；废弃的
qualified	/ˈkwɒlɪfaɪd/	adj.	有资格的；合格的
scrap	/skræp/	v.	报废；废弃
hydrolyze	/ˈhaɪdrəlaɪz/	v.	水解
cascade	/kæsˈkeɪd/	n.	级联
circular	/ˈsɜːkjʊlər/	adj.	圆形的；循环的
outlet	/ˈaʊtlet/	n.	出口；销售点

 ## Phrases and Expressions

phosphorus pentafluoride	五氟化磷
hydrogen fluoride	氟化氢
non-ferrous metal	有色金属
national standards for NEV	新能源汽车国家标准
cascade utilization	级联利用
material recovery	材料回收
environmental pollution	环境污染
economic opportunity	经济机会
circular economy	循环经济

recycling industry	回收产业
qualified enterprise	合格企业
resource security	资源安全

Reading 2　How Well Can Electric Vehicle Batteries Be Recycled?

Millions of electric vehicles are now being sold around the world, containing large lithium-ion batteries. For reasons of both safety and sustainability, these batteries must be recycled or carefully disposed of when the cars reach the end of their driving lives.

Elsa Olivetti, Jerry McAfee (1940) Professor in Engineering in the Department of Materials Science and Engineering (DMSE), says that like all forms of recycling, the EV battery recycling business will be driven by which materials are most profitable to salvage. In the case of lithium-ion batteries, she says, that most often means metals such as nickel and cobalt. These materials are expensive and often mined in lower-income countries under problematic conditions.

Recycling nickel and cobalt from old batteries could decrease the need for new mining, particularly if recyclers can recover over 95% of these materials as claimed. However, as the world transitions from gas-powered to electric vehicles, the demand for these materials will far outpace the supply from recycling, so mining metals such as cobalt will still be necessary.

To be recycled, EV batteries must first be dismantled, which is no simple task because batteries are not standardized. The packs from a Tesla, BMW, and Nissan EV are different sizes, containing differently-shaped battery cells joined together by welds and other connections that must be broken down. This complexity makes the process more expensive and dangerous.

"The significant challenge in battery recycling is the variability in chemistry and form factor, and that we have to be cautious to discharge them when they are recovered," Olivetti says. That's especially important because old or broken lithium-ion batteries can catch fire, which adds to the danger of stockpiling them for disposal.

Once the old batteries are taken apart, there are several possible methods for materials recycling. "Pyrometallurgical" processes subject the materials to very high temperatures in a furnace to recover some of the component metals. "Hydrometallurgical" processes subject the battery parts to chemical solutions dissolved in water to leach out the desired metals. Neither method is perfect: pyrometallurgical recycling uses a lot of energy, while hydrometallurgical recycling requires components to be broken down even further beforehand.

It's possible that many electric car batteries will be reused, not recycled. An older EV battery may no longer be useful for long-distance driving but could still have enough storage capacity to find a second life elsewhere. For example, Olivetti says, blocks of old batteries could be used to ease strain on the power grid by providing **backup** electricity when it's needed most. In 2018, Nissan experimented with this idea by using new and old batteries from their Leaf EV model to power the Ajax Amsterdam soccer stadium. "But we have to be sure we understand the state of the battery's health," Olivetti says. "And that's a challenge."

 ## New Words

profitable	/'prɒfɪtəbl/	*adj.*	有利可图的
salvage	/'sælvɪdʒ/	*v.*	抢救；回收利用
outpace	/aʊt'peɪs/	*v.*	超过；快于
dismantle	/dɪs'mæntl/	*v.*	拆卸；拆除
variability	/ˌveərɪə'bɪlɪti/	*n.*	变化性；可变性
discharge	/dɪs'tʃɑːdʒ/	*v.*	放电；排放
recover	/rɪ'kʌvə/	*v.*	回收；恢复
stockpile	/'stɒk,paɪl/	*v.*	储存；囤积
pyrometallurgical	/ˌpaɪrəmə'tælədʒɪkəl/	*adj.*	火法冶金的
furnace	/'fɜːnɪs/	*n.*	熔炉；火炉
component	/kəm'pəʊnənt/	*n.*	组件；成分
hydrometallurgical	/ˌhaɪdrəmə'tælədʒɪkəl/	*adj.*	湿法冶金的
leach	/liːtʃ/	*v.*	过滤；浸出
backup	/'bækʌp/	*n.*	备用；后备

 ## Phrases and Expressions

battery recycling	电池回收
component metals	组件金属
pyrometallurgical process	火法冶金工艺
hydrometallurgical process	湿法冶金工艺
reused, not recycled	再利用，而不是回收
electric vehicle battery	电动汽车电池

| power grid | 电网 |
| backup electricity | 备用电力 |

Speaking Activity: Exploring Battery Recycling in China and the US

Step 1: Reading Comprehension

(1) Read the assigned text about battery recycling in China or the US.

(2) Highlight key information about the recycling processes, challenges, and opportunities.

(3) Write down 2–3 questions you have about battery recycling in the other country.

Step 2: Jigsaw Groups

(1) Form a group with students who read about the other country.

(2) Share a summary of the key information from your reading.

(3) Ask your prepared questions and discuss the similarities and differences between battery recycling in China and the US.

(4) As a group, identify 2–3 best practices or innovative solutions from each country.

Step 3: Recycling Poster

(1) Return to your original groups.

(2) Collaborate to make a poster explaining the battery recycling process, challenges, opportunities and best practices in your assigned country.

(3) Include visuals and a catchy slogan to encourage recycling.

(4) Prepare a 2-minute presentation to introduce your poster.

Step 4: Poster Presentation

(1) Display your group's poster at the front of the classroom.

(2) Give a 2-minute presentation to introduce your poster to the class.

(3) Respond to questions and feedback from your classmates.

(4) Take notes on the other group's poster and presentation.

Step 5: Reflection

(1) Individually, write a short reflection on what you learned:

- What was most surprising or interesting about battery recycling in the other country?

- What best practices could be applied in your country?

- Why is intercultural understanding important for addressing global sustainability issues?

(2) If time allows, share highlights from your reflection with a partner or the whole class.

PART III Understanding Global Issues

Directions: Discuss the following questions with your group members. Note down the key information and share your insights with the entire class.

(1) What is your understanding of recycling?

(2) What challenges do you face when you try to recycle?

(3) In what ways has recycling made a positive impact on the environment?

(4) What do you think the future of recycling will look like in the next 20 years?

PART IV Developing Intercultural Communication Competence

Activity 1   Sharing Movies on Intercultural Communication

Directions: In your groups, each member is invited to share a movie involving intercultural communication that you have watched. Provide some background information about the movie and identify the intercultural communication scenarios. Below is an introduction to the film "The Gua Sha Treatment (《刮痧》)."

The Gua Sha Treatment, directed by Xiaolong Zheng, is a Chinese drama film that explores the cultural clash between Eastern and Western medical practices. The story revolves around a Chinese immigrant family in the United States. When the grandfather uses Gua Sha, a traditional Chinese healing technique, on his grandson, the resulting marks lead American authorities to suspect child abuse. This misunderstanding highlights the significant differences in cultural perspectives on healthcare and family practices. The film delves into themes of cultural identity, the immigrant experience, and the challenges of navigating between two distinct cultural worlds. Through its narrative, *The Gua Sha Treatment* underscores the importance of cultural competence and understanding in an increasingly globalized society.

Activity 2   What Really Happened?

Directions: *Discuss your understanding of the following scenarios from "The Gua Sha Treatment" and explain in your own words how to resolve the intercultural miscommunication presented.*

Scenario 1:

Xu Datong slapped his son, Dennis, in front of his boss Quinlin because Dennis had a fight with the boss's child, and the boss was his good friend. The boss couldn't understand why Xu Datong hit Dennis.

At the hearing, Datong's boss testified that Datong had hit Dennis, which left Datong extremely disappointed and angry, leading him to end both his friendship and professional relationship with the boss. In a subsequent conversation, Datong revealed the reason for hitting his son.

Datong: I considered you as my friend, but you sold me out. How could you ask me to work with you again?

Quinlin: I just told the truth. You shouldn't hit Dennis.

Datong: Why I hit him? Why? My own son? I hit him to show my respect for you. To give you face. You know?

Quinlin: What kind of twisted Chinese logic is that! You have to hit your own son so you can show your respect to me?

Datong: 不可理喻。

Quinlin: What did you say?

Datong: Okay. Let me share this final Chinese proverb with you. 道不同不相为谋。

Scenario 2:

In court, when Xu Datong attempts to explain Gua Sha, he has to use Chinese terms like "Tan Tien" and "Seven Jin and Eight Mai" because there are no corresponding terms in English, leaving the Americans completely baffled.

Datong: I think you don't understand. You know Gua Sha is a traditional Chinese medical treatment, used for nearly all kinds of illnesses. For thousands of years, Chinese medicine recognized that there are "Seven Jing and Eight Mai". An example. It's like small streams that run into rivers and then into seas. A person's body has an invisible but very complex system of vessel network, just like the computer network. And also, the human "Qi" from Tan Tien, finally goes through Tan Tien, which is the same principle.

PART V Introduction to the Course Project

Quality Control and Final Review

Before moving on to distribution, an essential step is conducting a quality control check and final review of your short video. This ensures that the video is polished and ready for your audience. Below are some tips.

(1) **Technical Review**

- Video Quality: Ensure all footage is clear and free from glitches.

- Audio Quality: Check for consistent volume levels and clarity. Ensure there are no background noises or audio sync issues.

- Visual Consistency: Confirm that color correction and grading are consistent across all scenes.

(2) **Content Review**

- Script and Dialogue: Verify that all spoken content aligns with your script and there are no errors or omissions.

- Graphics and Titles: Ensure all text elements are correctly spelled and placed appropriately.

- Pacing and Flow: Watch the entire video to check the pacing and make sure the transitions are smooth.

(3) **Feedback Session**

- Peer Review: Have classmates or peers watch the video and provide feedback.

- Instructor Review: If possible, get feedback from your instructor to ensure the video meets academic standards.

(4) Final Edits

- Incorporate Feedback: Make necessary adjustments based on the feedback received.

- Final Watch-Through: Do a complete viewing to confirm that all changes have been implemented and the video is polished.

(5) Final Touches

- Consistency Check: Ensure the video is consistent in terms of style, tone, and quality.

- Backup: Save your final project files and exported video in multiple locations to prevent data loss.

Unit 8

Green Development

Quiz 8

Learning Objectives:

After studying this unit, you should be able to

● develop a comprehensive understanding of green development on a global scale;

● analyze and reflect on your real-world intercultural communication experiences;

● expand your short video's reach to a wider audience.

PART I Listening and Speaking

Section 1 Pre-Listening Activity

Directions: *Discuss the following questions with your classmates. List the key information, and prepare to share your opinion with the class.*

(1) What are the key components of green development?

(2) How do green products influence consumer choices? Do you think people are more likely to buy environmentally friendly products? Share an example to show the impact of green products on consumer behavior.

(3) How can communities come together to implement green initiatives locally, such as community gardens, recycling programs, or energy-saving projects?

(4) How important is innovation in achieving green development? What are some recent technological advancements that have made a significant impact?

(5) How can education systems be adapted to better prepare students for careers in green industries? Should environmental education be a mandatory part of the curriculum?

(6) Why is it important for countries to work together on green development? Can you give examples of successful international cooperation in this area?

Section 2 Listening Comprehension

Passage 1

Directions: *Listen to Passage 1 and choose the best answer to each question.*

(1) What is the primary goal of the Global Green Growth Institute (GGGI)?

A. Promoting global trade.

B. Advancing green development.

C. Increasing agricultural output.

D. Expanding digital infrastructure.

(2) How many member organizations does GGGI have worldwide?

A. 28.   B. 38.   C) 48.   D. 58.

(3) What is GGGI primarily focused on helping member countries achieve?

A. High economic growth.

B. Low-carbon economy.

C. Military advancements.

D. Education reform.

(4) Which country has announced a $3 million investment to support GGGI's projects?

A. China.   B. Sri Lanka.

C. United Arab Emirates.   D. Japan.

(5) With which country is GGGI seeking stronger cooperation to achieve a greener future?

A. India.   B. Sri Lanka.

C. United States.   D. Brazil.

(6) Who is the Director General of GGGI?

A. Ban Ki-moon.   B. Joe Biden.

C. Frank Rijsberman.   D. António Guterres.

(7) At which event did Frank Rijsberman discuss the role of green cooperation under the BRI framework?

A. United Nations Climate Change Conference.

B. World Economic Forum.

C. Boao Forum for Asia Annual Conference 2024.

D. G20 Summit.

(8) Which country's clean technology expertise and financial resources are seen as a game changer in the fight against the climate crisis?

A. The United States'.   B. Germany's.

C. Japan's.   D. China's.

(9) What industries did Rijsberman praise China for leading in?

A. Steel and construction.

B. Solar panels, electric vehicles, and batteries.

C. Agriculture and textiles.

D. Pharmaceuticals and biotech.

(10) Which aspect of the BRI framework does Frank Rijsberman emphasize as crucial for tackling global climate change?

A. Economic growth.

B. Military partnerships.

C. Zero-carbon transition of Asia's power system.

D. Cultural preservation.

Passage 2

1. Directions: Listen to Passage 2 and choose the best answer to each question.

(1) Which of the following factors has contributed most to the growth of patents in new-energy vehicles and solid-state batteries in China?

A. Decrease in consumer interest in green products.

B. Significant investments from Chinese companies in these technologies.

C. Reduced research and development spending by leading companies like NIO.

D. A shift away from intellectual property to focus on cost advantages.

(2) Which company holds the most invention patents in the new-energy vehicle industry?

A. Xiaomi.   B. Gree.   C. Haier.   D. NIO.

(3) Which new player in the EV market secured 60 patents in motor electronic control?

A. Gree.   B. NIO.   C. Xiaomi.   D. Haier.

(4) By which year does China aim to achieve carbon neutrality?

A. 2025.   B. 2030.   C. 2050.   D. 2060.

(5) How has the China National Intellectual Property Administration (CNIPA) supported the growth of green technologies?

A. By increasing the complexity of the patent review process.

B. By outsourcing patent reviews to international organizations.

C. By speeding up the review process for patents related to energy conservation and environmental protection.

D. By limiting the number of patents, a company can file each year.

2. Directions: *Listen to Passage 2 again and decide whether the statements are true (T) or false (F).*

(6) _____ China filed more than half of the world's green and low-carbon patents in 2023.

(7) _____ NIO spent 13.43 billion yuan on research and development in 2023.

(8) _____ Xiaomi is an established player in the EV market with many years of experience.

(9) _____ Gree has filed about 3,500 patents related to energy conservation.

(10) _____ China's younger consumers are less likely to prefer green products, according to the 2023 report.

PART **II** Reading and Speaking

Reading 1   Green Development in China

China's commitment to green development is paramount in the global climate transition. It introduced the strategic concept of 'Building a Beautiful China' in 2012, emphasizing ecological protection and sustainable resource utilization. President Xi Jinping's recent emphasis on harmonizing humanity with nature reinforces the nation's pledge to peak carbon emissions by 2030 and achieve carbon neutrality by 2060.

China has been continuously refining its energy structure, increasing the proportion of non-fossil energy sources. By the end of October 2023, renewable energy capacity exceeded coal power capacity, marking a historic moment. The target for 2024 is to elevate the share of non-fossil energy in total energy consumption to approximately 18.9%.

In transportation, China is committed to reducing the environmental pollution of traditional fuel vehicles and accelerating the development of the new energy vehicle industry. China witnessed a remarkable surge in the production and sales of new energy vehicles in 2023 and holds over 60% of the global market share, becoming a major driving force behind China's sustainability.

The fashion industry also strongly supports sustainability. Susan Fang, a Chinese fashion brand, has made sustainability a core part of its brand through the development of a zero-waste air-weave process and the use of transparent glass bead material for its popular bead bags. Beauty brands like Yue Sai practice sustainable development by extracting ingredients through bio-fermentation and green processes, utilizing environmentally friendly replaceable cores, and launching empty bottle recycling programs.

China's three major exchanges issued guidelines on sustainable development reporting for listed companies, requiring them to analyze and disclose sustainability issues across governance, strategy, impact, risk, and opportunity management. Implementation of these regulations can mitigate environmental risks, improve resource efficiency, reduce negative impacts, enhance corporate reputation, and drive long-term sustainability. Companies adhering to green development can benefit from government incentives and subsidies.

China's sustainability commitment is evidenced by its urban performance. By 2025, China aims to enforce waste sorting in all urban communities at the prefecture level and above. As of the end of 2022, the average garbage classification coverage rate in urban residential communities had reached 82.5%. China is also actively promoting green rural development through ecological protection and restoration efforts.

Despite its status as a major energy consumer, China remains committed to pursuing sustainable development. The country persists in refining its energy framework, supporting the new energy vehicle industry, enacting regulations for listed companies, and promoting urban garbage classification and rural ecological protection. As of 2024, significant investments in sustainable infrastructure and policies are driving forward China's ecological and economic goals.

New Words

paramount	/ˈpærəmaʊnt/	adj.	最重要的；至高无上的
transparent	/trænsˈpærənt/	adj.	透明的；清晰的
bio-fermentation	/ˌbaɪəʊˌfɜːmenˈteɪʃən/	n.	生物发酵

disclose	/dɪsˈkləʊz/	v.	披露；公开
governance	/ˈɡʌvənəns/	n.	治理；管理
incentive	/ɪnˈsentɪv/	n.	激励；刺激
prefecture	/ˈpriːfektʃə/	n.	地区；辖区

Phrases and Expressions

green development	绿色发展
carbon neutrality	碳中和
renewable energy capacity	可再生能源容量
new energy vehicle industry	新能源汽车产业
sustainable resource utilization	可持续资源利用
urban garbage classification	城市垃圾分类
rural ecological protection	农村生态保护
sustainable development reporting	可持续发展报告
waste sorting	垃圾分类
government incentive	政府激励措施

Reading 2   Singapore Green Plan 2030

The Singapore Green Plan 2030, launched in February 2021, is a comprehensive national strategy that sets forth Singapore's long-term goals for environmental sustainability over the next decade. This plan aims to transform Singapore into a sustainable and resilient city, **aligning** with global efforts such as the United Nations' 2030 Sustainable Development Agenda and the Paris Agreement.

The Green Plan addresses pressing environmental challenges, including climate change, biodiversity loss, and resource sustainability. It outlines ambitious targets, such as planting 1 million more trees, **quadrupling** solar energy deployment by 2025, and reducing waste sent to **landfills** by 30% by 2030. These targets aim to reduce Singapore's carbon footprint and enhance its environmental resilience.

The plan is significant for sustainability issues in Singapore and the broader Southeast Asian region. It seeks to mitigate the effects of climate change by reducing greenhouse gas emissions and improving air quality. The Green Plan also aims to make Singapore more **livable** and **resource-efficient** by reducing waste and promoting sustainable living practices. By demonstrating practical strategies for sustainable development, Singapore can inspire neighboring countries to adopt similar measures and drive regional efforts to combat climate change.

The Singapore Green Plan 2030 is structured around five key pillars: City in Nature, Sustainable Living, Energy Reset, Green Economy, and Resilient Future. The City in Nature pillar aims to develop Singapore's green spaces and promote urban biodiversity. Sustainable Living encourages eco-friendly practices and responsible resource consumption. Energy Reset focuses on transitioning to cleaner energy sources like solar power. The Green Economy pillar positions Singapore as a global leader in green finance and innovation. Lastly, Resilient Future prepares Singapore for the impacts of climate change through coastal protection infrastructure and climate-resilient urban planning.

Since its launch, the Green Plan has made significant progress, with notable achievements in solar energy capacity, car-lite zones, public education campaigns, community gardens, and green finance initiatives. However, implementing the plan also presents challenges, such as limited land space and balancing economic growth with environmental sustainability.

These challenges offer opportunities for innovation in sustainable technologies, regional collaboration, public-private partnerships, and raising public awareness. Future developments will focus on expanding green spaces, advancing renewable energy, strengthening climate resilience, and promoting sustainable business practices.

The success of the Green Plan relies on the collective efforts of the government, businesses, and the community. By working together and embracing sustainable practices, Singapore can serve as a model for other nations and create a greener, more sustainable world.

New Words

align	/əˈlaɪn/	v.	使一致；对齐
quadruple	/kwɒˈdruːpl/	v.	使成四倍；四倍增长
landfill	/ˈlændfɪl/	n.	垃圾填埋场
livable	/ˈlɪvəbl/	adj.	适宜居住的
resource-efficient	/rɪˈzɔːs ɪˈfɪʃənt/	adj.	资源高效的

Phrases and Expressions

coastal protection	海岸保护
collective effort	集体努力
eco-friendly practice	环保实践
green finance	绿色金融
energy reset	能源重置
waste reduction	减少废物
climate resilience	气候韧性
public education campaign	公共教育活动

Speaking Activity: Green Development in Singapore and China

Step 1: Form Groups and Assign Roles

(1) Form groups of 4–5 students, ensuring each group has a mix of students from different cultural backgrounds, if possible.

(2) Within each group, assign the following roles:

- Facilitator: Keeps the discussion on track and ensures equal participation

- Recorder: Takes notes during the discussion and summarizes key points

- Presenter: Presents the group's findings to the class

- Researcher(s): Conducts additional research on green development in Singapore and China, if needed

Step 2: Analyze and Compare

(1) Read the provided texts on green development in Singapore and China.

(2) Discuss and compare the key aspects of each country's approach to green development, considering factors such as:

- Goals and targets

- Key pillars or focus areas

- Progress and achievements

- Challenges and opportunities

(3) Identify similarities and differences between the two countries' strategies.

(4) Consider how cultural values, beliefs, and practices may influence each country's approach to green development.

Step 3: Reflect on Intercultural Communication

(1) Reflect on your own cultural background and how it may shape your perspective on green development.

(2) Share your personal experiences or knowledge related to sustainability and environmental issues in your own country or culture.

(3) Practice active listening and respectful communication while discussing potentially sensitive topics.

(4) Be open to learning from your group members' diverse perspectives and experiences.

Step 4: Brainstorm Solutions

(1) Brainstorm innovative solutions or best practices that Singapore and China could learn from each other to enhance their green development efforts.

(2) Consider how intercultural collaboration and knowledge-sharing could contribute to global sustainability goals.

(3) Discuss potential challenges in implementing these solutions and how they might be addressed.

Step 5: Present Findings and Engage in Class Discussion

(1) The Presenter from each group shares the group's key findings, including:

- Similarities and differences between Singapore's and China's green development strategies
- Reflections on how cultural factors may influence each country's approach
- Innovative solutions or best practices that could be shared between the two countries

(2) Engage in a class discussion, guided by the teacher, to further explore the topic and share insights from each group.

(3) Reflect on how this activity has enhanced your understanding of green development and intercultural communication competence.

PART **III** Understanding Global Issues

Directions: *Discuss the following questions with your group members. Note down the key information and share your insights with the entire class.*

(1) How does green development contribute to the well-being of people worldwide?

(2) Can you provide examples of successful international collaborations in green development?

(3) What lessons can be learned from traditional and indigenous practices around the world that support green development?

(4) How can green development address some global environmental challenges?

PART **IV** Developing Intercultural Communication Competence

Activity 1   Exploring Personal Experiences in Intercultural Communication

Directions: *Interview each other and share your personal experiences with intercultural communication. This could involve interactions with people from different cultures, whether through direct encounters or through media such as television, books, or social events.*

1. Interview with Each Other and Share Your Experience

- Who: Identify the individuals involved. Were they friends, strangers, colleagues, or people you encountered during travel, volunteering, or other activities?

- What: Share the story. What was the context of the interaction? Did it take place in a formal or informal setting? What was the main topic or focus of the communication (e.g., food, language, cultural practices)? Was it a successful intercultural communication experience?

- Conflict or Misunderstanding (if applicable): Did any conflicts, misunderstandings, or cultural differences arise during this interaction? If so, what were they?

- Resolution (if applicable): How did you or the others involved address the conflict/misunderstanding? What strategies or communication techniques were used to overcome the barriers?

2. Mind Mapping

Create a mind map to visually represent the intercultural communication experience. The mind map should include:

- Key aspects of the experience (people involved, cultural context, etc.)

- Any conflict or misunderstanding and its causes (if applicable)

- The strategies or methods used for resolution (if applicable)

- Lessons learned or insights gained from the experience

3. Presentation

Present your findings to the class. Your presentation should cover the story, the challenges faced, how they were addressed, and what was learned from the experience.

Activity 2   Reflection and Application

Direction: *First, review the key concepts and strategies of intercultural communication you've learned throughout the textbook. After that, write a short reflection (200-300 words) on what you gained from the previous activity, focusing on how it deepened your understanding of intercultural communication. Finally, consider how you can apply these concepts and skills to a real-world intercultural communication situation, such as engaging in a community event, participating in a cultural exchange program, volunteering with an international organization, joining a language exchange, or even interacting through virtual platforms if in-person opportunities are not available.*

PART Ⅴ Introduction to the Course Project

Sharing with a Broader Audience

After the meticulous process of post-production, the next crucial step is ensuring that your short video reaches its intended audience. By carefully selecting the right platforms, optimizing your content, actively promoting it, and engaging with viewers, you can significantly increase your video's visibility. Here are some tips to help you effectively share the final product:

(1) Choose the Right Platform

- Video Sharing Sites: Upload the video to popular platforms that cater to the target audience.

- Social Media: Share the video on social media networks to reach a broader audience and encourage sharing.

(2) Optimize the Video

- Title and Description: Craft an engaging title and write a detailed description, incorporating relevant keywords to improve the video's searchability.

- Thumbnails: Design an eye-catching thumbnail that effectively represents the content and entices viewers to click.

- Tags and Metadata: Use appropriate tags and metadata to enhance the video's discoverability across different platforms.

(3) Share and Promote

- Cross-Promotion: Share the video across various social media platforms and engage in relevant online communities where the content will resonate.

- Collaborations: Partner with influencers or other content creators to tap into their audience and expand your reach.

(4) Engage with Your Audience

- Comments and Feedback: Actively respond to comments and interact with the viewers to build a community around the content.

- Analytics: Use analytics tools to monitor the video's performance, gain insights into viewer behavior, and make data-driven improvements to future content.